DATE DUE

UNDER 21

UNDER 21

A YOUNG PEOPLE'S GUIDE
TO LEGAL RIGHTS

BY
MICHAEL DORMAN

DELACORTE PRESS / NEW YORK, N. Y.

Second Printing – 1971

For Pam and Trish,
who usually assert their rights responsibly (if loudly)

CONTENTS

1

YOUNG PEOPLE
HAVE RIGHTS TOO!

IN Des Moines, Iowa, two high school students and a junior high student, in defiance of a ban by school authorities, wore black armbands to class as a protest against the Vietnam war. As a result, they were suspended from school. But the U.S. Supreme Court later ruled the suspensions were illegal, holding that the First Amendment to the Constitution protects the rights of public school children to express their political and social views during school hours.

In Gila County, Arizona, a fifteen-year-old boy was arrested after being accused of making an obscene telephone call to a woman neighbor. A juvenile court judge ruled the boy was a juvenile delinquent and committed him to a reform school. The juvenile court proceedings, following what had become relatively standard procedures up to that time, denied the boy some of the rights that would have been routinely granted if he had been an adult. Among them were the right to be provided with a court-appointed attorney if his family could not afford to hire a lawyer, the right to have his attorney cross-examine witnesses, and the right to avoid being forced to incriminate himself. The U.S. Supreme Court ruled that the juvenile court acted unconstitutionally in denying the boy those rights.

In Williams Bay, Wisconsin, a sixteen-year-old boy was suspended from high school for defying a rule against long hair. The boy took his case to court. A federal district court judge ruled that the ban on long hair was unconstitutional.

He ordered school authorities to reinstate the student immediately, to remove all mention of the disciplinary action from the boy's school records, and to refrain from enforcing the long-hair regulation in the future. The Supreme Court later sustained his ruling.

In Stony Brook, New York, the student governing body at the local campus of the State University of New York took the unusual step of hiring an attorney to represent the student body in its dealings with the university administration. The attorney was assigned to investigate the legality of certain administration policies and to "define relationships between administration, faculty, and students."

In Boston, Massachusetts, a young man received his notice to report for the military draft. He sought exemption from the draft on the ground that he was a conscientious objector. His draft board informed him that the Selective Service Act granted conscientious-objector status only to someone who "by reason of religious training and belief is conscientiously opposed to participation in war in any form." The young man did not meet those criteria. His objection to war was not based on a formal religion, but rather on an informal set of moral and ethical values. Moreover, he objected specifically to the Vietnam war—not necessarily to all wars. Despite the limitation in the law, the young man refused to accept military induction. He was then convicted of violating the draft law. But a federal district judge later overturned the conviction. He declared unconstitutional the section of the draft law requiring a conscientious objector to be opposed on religious grounds to all wars.

In Greenville, South Carolina, a group of young soldiers organized a meeting at the Army's Fort Jackson training base to express opposition to the Vietnam war. The soldiers

[4]

were arrested and imprisoned in the base stockade, charged with the "serious [military] offense" of speaking out publicly against the war. They then filed suit against the Army, seeking to obtain for GIs the same rights of protest that civilians enjoy under the First Amendment to the Constitution.

These cases illustrate a significant new trend in American life. Young people, particularly those under twenty-one years of age, are demanding that they be granted rights long denied them as a matter of course. And, with increasing frequency, they are winning those rights.

The relationships of young people to other members of American society and to society's established institutions are undergoing a period of upheaval. New answers are being found to questions that were rarely even posed until recently. Long-standing rules and attitudes are being reversed. These changes are occurring over a broad spectrum —including the rights of minors in relation to their parents, schools, government, employers, military authorities, and society generally. In growing numbers, young people are forsaking blind obedience to their elders and asking: "What are our rights in this situation?"

What right, for example, does a young man or woman have to run away from home or drop out of school?

What right does he have to publish unpopular views, despite school authorities' disapproval, in a school newspaper?

What right does he have to wear unorthodox clothing or long hair in school?

What right does he have to enter into a contract, such as an agreement to buy an automobile, and what responsibilities does he assume under the contract?

[5]

What rights does he have when arrested? Do these rights differ from those of an adult?

What rights does he have in seeking deferment from the military draft? How have these rights changed recently?

Once in military service, what right does he have to protest against government policies?

What rights does a student have to demonstrate political views during school hours or on school property?

What right does a minor have to marry, in spite of parents' objections?

These are some of the questions receiving increased attention as young people move to assert their independence. The questions, however, merely scratch the surface of a complex subject. Each question, in turn, raises others. Answers are often hard to come by. Too often in the past, issues concerning the rights of young people were either ignored or distorted. Thus, it is little wonder that many minors and adults are confused about the legal rights of persons under twenty-one years of age.

This book is an attempt to clear away as much of the confusion as possible and to provide the young reader with a practical guide. While laws vary from state to state and some court decisions appear to be in conflict with others, fundamental guidelines covering the rights of minors are emerging on a national basis. An examination of the national pattern should enable responsible young people to reach sound conclusions on just how far their rights extend and how best to go about exercising them.

STUDENT RIGHTS: DRESS AND HAIRSTYLE

THE place where more young Americans are asserting their rights than any other is undoubtedly the school. The exercise of these rights takes many forms, including the protest demonstration, the publication in the school newspaper of editorials critical of school administrators, the expression of political views during school hours, and the wearing of long hair or clothing styles frowned upon by school authorities. Of these, the issue that creates perhaps the most frequent clashes between students and their elders is the hair-clothing question.

There is a tendency on the part of many adults to regard students' clothing and hair styles lightly, as matters of little importance. But, to the students themselves, these are issues of great consequence. Attempts by school administrators to enforce rigid hair and clothing codes are viewed by students as representative of intended regimentation in other fields as well. Thus, their insistence on wearing the forbidden styles often is symbolic of their more general determination to see that their rights are recognized across the board.

A recent attempt to place the hair-clothing issue in perspective was made by Spencer Coxe, executive director of the Philadelphia branch of the American Civil Liberties Union.

Coxe explored the legal aspects of the hair-clothing question. He pointed out that the American legal system permits a government agency, including a school, to do only those things that are authorized by an act of the legislature. If the legislature has not given the schools the power to prescribe hairstyles, Coxe asserted, then the schools cannot do so—no matter how strongly a principal or teacher may feel.

Of course, the fifty states have fifty different school laws that differ at least somewhat in language and intent. But Coxe said he felt the Pennsylvania law, the one with which he was most familiar, was fairly typical of the national pattern. The Pennsylvania law gives school authorities "the right to exercise the same authority as to *conduct* and *behavior* over the pupils attending school . . . during the time they are in attendance . . . as the parents may exercise over them." The American Civil Liberties Union's interpretation of the Pennsylvania law is that the school has no right to tell a student how to wear his hair, since hairstyle is neither "conduct" nor "behavior."

School officials often argue that they are compelled to ban unorthodox hair and clothing styles in order to maintain student discipline. Such was the case when a fifteen-year-old student, David Harris, was suspended from his junior high school in Haverford, Pennsylvania, for wearing a Prince Charles haircut. The local school board upheld the suspension, ruling that "the condition of the boy's hair obviously would tend to be a threat against reasonable discipline." But Coxe assailed this logic, charging that what the board contended was "obvious" was actually far from obvious. One of the major problems with school dress and hair regulations, Coxe pointed out, is that they invariably include terms—such as "good grooming," "acceptable" and "extreme"—subject to various interpretations.

Perhaps the most important argument against hair and

dress codes is that hair and clothing styles are forms of personal expression protected by the First Amendment to the Constitution. "Many young people wear their hair the way they do because it helps them express their individuality," Coxe says. "To many adults, such a form of expression may seem pretty foolish; still, it is protected, along with other nonconformist expressions, by the Constitution. After all, adults are allowed to wear paper hats and make fools of themselves at New Year's Eve parties."

Questions on the constitutionality of such codes, however, have been decided in different ways by different courts; the U.S. Supreme Court has not yet ruled on the issues. Thus, it is impossible to set down guides that will cover every situation in every state. But consideration of rulings by various courts and state education officials does provide insight into trends developing across the country. Not surprisingly, New York State—long a hotbed of activity by civil liberties advocates—has been the site of several cases worthy of examination.

One such case revolved around a decision by a high school principal in Saratoga Springs, New York, suspending a female student for defying a ban on wearing slacks to school. The student, a high school senior named Sharon Ann Dalrymple, wore the slacks on a day when the temperature was six degrees above zero. She had recently been ill. She was obliged to walk more than a mile from her home to school. Moreover, her school consisted of several buildings—so she was compelled to go outdoors in changing classes. In view of all these factors, Sharon's mother directed her to wear slacks both to school and during school. The principal promptly suspended Sharon and sent her home, telling her not to return until she could comply with the ban. His ruling was upheld by the local school board.

Sharon's mother, Mrs. Patricia Dalrymple, appealed the suspension to New York State Commissioner of Education James E. Allen, Jr. (later appointed U.S. Commissioner of Education). Allen, after considering the evidence, ruled that school districts had the power to make *reasonable rules* concerning students' appearance while in school, but that the Saratoga Springs ban on slacks was not reasonable.

The test of reasonableness, Allen held, would give school boards the clear right, for example, "to prohibit the wearing of such items as metal cleats on the shoes which might damage the floors, a type of clothing in physical education classes which unduly restricts the student from participating [in athletics], long-haired angora sweaters in cooking classes where open-flame gas ranges were used, any kind of apparel which indecently exposes the body or, in sum, any clothing which causes a disturbance in the classroom, endangers the student, or is so distractive as to interfere with the learning and teaching process." While ruling that Sharon's wearing of slacks did not violate such provisions, Allen stopped short of overruling her suspension. Instead, he sent the case back to the school board for further action. Sharon was eventually readmitted.

Despite the fact that it did not go so far as some students and civil liberties advocates would have liked, this decision was a significant one. It prepared the way for a series of later rulings that were considerably more far-reaching in spelling out students' rights to dress as they choose.

For example, six months after ruling on Sharon's case, Commissioner Allen was called upon to decide the case of another student ousted from school over a clothing dispute.

The student, Joseph McQuade, Jr., a tenth-grader at Shaker High School in Colonie, New York, was suspended because he and his parents insisted that he wear a certain type of footwear to school. School authorities, in defending their suspension order, described the footwear as "an extreme type of western-style boots." Commissioner Allen, after examining the "boots" at a hearing in the case, said they appeared to be plain black shoes, somewhat above ankle height, with heavy zipper fasteners on the sides, pointed toes, and approximately one-and-a-half-inch heels.

Testimony at the hearing disclosed that several of Joseph's teachers had told him the shoes were not proper school attire and had suggested that he wear conventional sneakers or loafers. When he continued to wear the shoes, he was suspended. In deciding the case, Allen referred specifically to his ruling in Sharon Dalrymple's case—particularly the section referring to a school board's right to prohibit the wearing of clothing that causes a disturbance in the classroom, endangers a student, or is so distracting that it interferes with the learning process.

He held there was no conclusive evidence in Joseph McQuade's case that the student's shoes met any of these criteria. "The [hearing] record merely indicates that the teachers do not like the style of the shoes," Allen wrote. "Hence, there is no legal basis to support the action of the school officials in refusing to permit this student to attend regular classes."

Moreover, the education commissioner noted, Shaker High School did not even have an established set of standards on student dress and appearance. Therefore, if Joseph's suspension were upheld, he and other students would be expected to abide by the individual, perhaps capricious, clothing tastes of scores of teachers. Allen overruled Joseph's suspension and ordered the school board to reinstate him immediately.

When Allen left his post as New York State's education commissioner to become U.S. education commissioner in President Nixon's administration, he was succeeded in the state post by Ewald B. Nyquist. And Nyquist proceeded to broaden still further the rights of New York students to dress and wear their hair as they please. In a series of decisions, he ordered the reinstatement of students barred from classes or school activities because of their appearance.

In one case a student named Jeffrey Myers was dropped from the basketball team at Pavilion Central High School in Genesee County for refusing to get a haircut. Nyquist ruled that the basketball coach had no right to drop a player for such a reason, and ordered Jeffrey restored to the team. "There is no way of showing that the length of the boy's hair in any way diminished his effectiveness as a basketball player," the commissioner ruled.

Another student, Daniel Cossey, was suspended from Linton High School in Schenectady for wearing his hair longer than was permitted by a dress code drawn up by the school's faculty, administration, and student body. The issue in the case, Nyquist wrote, was whether a matter such as hairstyle "was subject to legally enforceable regulations in accordance with the wishes of the majority." Ruling that it was not, the commissioner said: "I hold that, since this dress code is concerned solely with questions of taste, its provisions are not enforceable by disciplinary action against a student who fails to abide by them."

Similarly, Nyquist ordered the reinstatement of two Port Chester High School students, Barbara Johnson and

Yvonne Watkins, who had been suspended for wearing slacks to school. He found that "there had been no allegations that the slacks worn had offended decency or that any disruption was occasioned."

The commissioner, in overruling the school authorities in each of these cases, served notice that the only dress codes he would consider enforceable would be those that related "to specific educational purposes of health, safety, and full participation in various activities." He further said: "The standards of taste of a previous generation are an insufficient basis for the imposition of restrictions upon students of today."

The New York branch of the Amercian Civil Liberties Union, whose lawyers represented the students in the cases decided by Nyquist, said the commissioner's rulings "once and for all make it clear that public school principals and superintendents have no power to suspend or otherwise discipline students for what the school considers improper dress." But subsequent events made it clear that some school administrators in New York State did not concur with the ACLU's assessment. Despite Nyquist's rulings, various school districts throughout the state continued to enforce dress codes based on questions of taste, rather than on "specific educational purposes of health, safety, and full participation in various activities." Under the law, Nyquist had no power to block enforcement of such codes until he received specific appeals from parents whose children had been disciplined. Thus, in order to enjoy the rights that Nyquist had already ruled were theirs, students in recalcitrant school districts were compelled to violate the dress codes and face the possibility of at least temporary suspensions or expulsions. Their parents were then obliged to go through the time-consuming, sometimes costly process of appealing to the education commissioner to overrule each individual disciplinary action. Such circumstances made it clear that, although they had won several significant victories in the fight against restrictive dress codes, New York students were still short of their goal.

New York students were far from alone in challenging school regulations on dress and hair styles. Their efforts were matched by their counterparts in other states throughout the country. One case that arose in California was considered particularly significant; it was later cited by legal experts in various other states as justification for liberalized dress codes. The case involved the refusal of high school authorities in Arcata, California, to admit a male student whose hair style they considered "extreme."

The boy's parents, aided by attorneys from the American Civil Liberties Union, took the case to court. They contended that the school regulation prohibiting "extreme" haircuts was unconstitutionally vague. California Superior Court Judge W. G. Watson agreed, and ordered the school officials to admit the student. "The limits within which regulations can be made by the school are that there be some reasonable connection to school matters, deportment, discipline, etc., or to the health and safety of the students," Judge Watson ruled. "The court has too high a regard for the school system . . . to think that they (educators) are aiming at uniformity or blind conformity as a means of achieving their stated goal in educating for responsible citizenship. Certainly, the school would be the first to concede that in a society as advanced as that in which we live there is room for many personal preferences, and great care should be exercised insuring that what are mere personal preferences of one are not forced upon another for mere convenience, since absolute uniformity among our citizens should be our last desire."

The school officials in Arcata, however, were unwilling to let the matter drop without a further fight. They appealed Judge Watson's decision to the California Court of Appeals. The ACLU attorneys argued before the Court of Appeals that hair fashion is a form of symbolic expression protected by the Constitution. Upholding this theory, the court sustained Judge Watson's decision and barred the school from enforcing its hairstyle regulations.

Another significant case arose in Williams Bay, Wisconsin. High school authorities there imposed a regulation that provided: "Boys' hair should be washed, combed, and worn so it does not hang below the collar line in the back, over the ears on the side and must be above the eyebrows. Boys should be clean-shaven; long sideburns are out."

Two boys with long hair, one sixteen years old and the other seventeen, were suspended from school for violating the regulation. The seventeen-year-old was readmitted when he got a haircut, but the sixteen-year-old refused to cut his hair and was denied reinstatement. ACLU attorneys, on behalf of both students, appealed the case first to the Wisconsin superintendent of public instruction. The superintendent upheld the school regulation, ruling that long hair "constitutes a disruption in the school and warrants expulsion."

Next, the case was taken to the court of U.S. District Judge James E. Doyle. He ruled in favor of the students, becoming the first federal judge to declare that a high school ban on long hair was unconstitutional. Judge Doyle held that the ban violated the Fourteenth Amendment's guarantees of due process of law, which are designed to protect citizens against arbitrary government actions providing no systematic method of determining justice. The judge ordered the school to reinstate the sixteen-year-old student immediately and to allow the seventeen-year-old to let his hair grow. He directed the school officials to stop enforcing the long-hair ban and to delete from their records any mention of the disciplinary action previously taken against the two students.

Judge Doyle said in his written decision that he disagreed with some other courts' characterization of the long-hair issue as political or social. Instead, he wrote, personal grooming "is a freedom deserving a high degree of protection." He cited testimony that, contrary to the claims of the school officials, the length of the two students' hair was not a distracting influence in the classroom. The time has come, Judge Doyle wrote, "to broaden the constitutional community by including within its protection younger people whose claim to dignity matches that of their elders." His decision was upheld by the Supreme Court.

Judge Doyle's ruling was soon echoed by several other federal judges. In Chicago, U.S. District Judge James B. Parsons ordered the suburban Barrington Consolidated High School to reinstate a student suspended for wearing long hair and a moustache. The student, seventeen-year-old David Miller, had followed the Wisconsin pattern by contending that his school's dress code was unconstitutional. In ordering David's reinstatement, Judge Parsons wrote that "a new day" had dawned in education. "We cannot mold the people of today in the mold of the people of the nineteen-twenties and the nineteen-thirties," he said. "We can't mold the people who are going to run the world in the nineteen-eighties in the shape of the nineteen-twenties. You just can't expect to make the future look like the past." In Boston, U.S. District Judge Charles E. Wyzanski issued a similar ruling in the case of a long-haired student suspended by the Marlboro High School. Wyzanski held that that there was no reason for the suspension, "except possibly the school principal's personal prejudice."

In Alabama, a student was suspended for wearing his hair in a "block" style, in violation of a school district regulation requiring boys' hair to be "shingled" or "tapered." The U.S. District Court for the Middle District of Alabama ordered the student reinstated.

It should not be assumed that all recent decisions have been in favor of liberalizing or eliminating school dress codes. While the tendency has been in that direction, there have nonetheless been quite a few rulings upholding the right of school officials to enforce strict dress and hairstyle regulations.

The Massachusetts State Supreme Court, for example, sustained a ban on long hair imposed by the school district in Attleboro. The court declined to consider constitutional questions raised by opponents of the ban, saying that it would review only the issue of whether some rational basis could be found for the short-hair rule. Concluding that unusual hairstyles could disrupt and impede the maintenance of proper classroom decorum, the court upheld the right of the district to suspend students for violating the ban.

A similar ruling was issued by a majority of judges on the U.S. Fifth Circuit Court of Appeals in a case involving the the school district in Dallas, Texas. The principal of a Dallas high school, testifying in support of regulations barring long hair, said that long-haired boys at the school had been challenged to a fight by other students. He also testified that considerable obscene language had been directed at the long-haired students by other boys. The principal's solution to the problem was to suspend the long-haired students from school. The appeals court majority upheld the principal's action, ruling that activity that hinders the state in providing the best possible education for its students must be eliminated or restricted if necessary. A strong dissenting opinion was filed by Judge Elbert P. Tuttle. "It is these acts [of harassment] that should be prohibited—not the expressions of individuality by the suspended students," Judge Tuttle wrote.

The U.S. Supreme Court sustained on June 1, 1970, the right of two Wisconsin school boys to wear their hair long. Robert W. Warren, Wisconsin attorney general, had contended public school students do not have a personal, fundamental right of free choice of grooming and dress. But the appeal was turned down unanimously. This leaves in effect decisions by lower courts that officials in Williams Bay, Wisconsin, could not discipline Thomas Breen and James Anton for wearing their hair long.

In view of these conflicting decisions, it is understandable that many students remain unclear about their rights in relation to dress and hairstyle codes. There are obviously no hard and fast rules covering all situations in all schools throughout the country. But some trends are emerging on a national basis.

One significant trend is the very willingness of courts to consider cases involving challenges of school codes on appearance. Until recently, many courts refused even to take up such matters, contending they were solely within the discretion of school authorities. Another current trend involves the tendency of the courts to place a heavy burden on the schools to justify their regulations on appearance. Generally, the courts compel the schools to prove that enforcement of their appearance codes is necessary in order to meet at least one of two basic criteria. These criteria are, first, protection of the health and welfare of the individual student and, second, the need to prevent disruption that would directly interfere with the teaching process. Unless one or both of these criteria can be clearly met, it is unlikely that a court will uphold the enforcement of an appearance code.

Thus, any student attending a school with a dress code that does not meet at least one of these standards can be reasonably confident in challenging the regulations. He should be aware, however, that the challenge may involve a lengthy, perhaps costly series of legal contests. A student who doubts the legitimacy of his school's code would be wise to seek guidance from the nearest office of the American Civil Liberties Union. The ACLU has affiliates in forty-one states and the District of Columbia. The address of the closest affiliate office can be obtained by writing to ACLU headquarters, 156 Fifth Avenue, New York, New York 10010.

SUMMARY

1. Most decisions by courts and statewide education officials recognize that, within limits, students have the right to dress and wear their hair as they and their parents wish.

2. The limits placed by school authorities that will be upheld by the courts generally must refer either to the health or well-being of the student or the need to prevent disruption that would interfere with the educational process.

3. If restrictions are to be placed on student dress, it is best to have a written code prepared with the cooperation of students, teachers, parents, and administrators. In some cases, however, even such codes may be held to violate individual students' rights.

4. Decisions by courts in various jurisdictions differ, so no student can be guaranteed that a ruling in another locality will necessarily be applicable to his case.

STUDENT RIGHTS:
THE RIGHT OF EXPRESSION

$\mathcal{S}$TUDENTS' assertion of the right to dress as they please is representative of their broader demands for school authorities to recognize their rights on a wide range of issues. They want, for example, clear recognition of their right to discuss in school any subject, no matter how controversial, that they feel is worthy of consideration. They want the freedom to publish uncensored school newspapers and magazines. They want the right to express political views during school hours and while participating in extracurricular activities on school grounds. They want reasonable access to such school communications media as the bulletin board and the public address system. They want the right to distribute handbills and other literature on school grounds. They want the right to make orderly protests, without fear of reprisal, against what they consider objectionable school policies. They want truly democratic student governments, free from unreasonable interference by teachers or administrators. They want due process to be followed by school authorities in maintaining discipline. In short, students want to be granted within the school rights comparable to those generally accorded adult citizens in everyday life.

Most American school districts have moved in recent years, with varying degrees of enthusiasm, in the direction of expanding student rights. Some have done so more or less voluntarily, others only under the pressure of lawsuits. Still others, resisting the national trend, have not budged at all thus far. But it is doubtful they will be able to continue withstanding change indefinitely. The tides—in the form of student activism, court decisions, and other influences—appear to be running against them.

Among the court rulings that have proved significant in liberalizing student rights, one of the most notable involved a case in Des Moines, Iowa. The case arose when several Des Moines students, with the support of their parents, decided to demonstrate their opposition to the Vietnam war and their support for a truce by wearing black armbands to school. The principals of the city's schools became aware of the student plan and met to decide how to cope with it. After the meeting, the principals announced that any student wearing an armband to school would be asked to remove it. If he refused, he would be suspended until he returned without an armband.

In spite of the ban, a number of students went through with the plan and wore the armbands to school. Among them were Christopher Eckhardt, sixteen, and John F. Tinker, fifteen, both high school students, and John's thirteen-year-old sister, Mary Beth Tinker, a junior high student. The wearing of the armbands caused no disruption of normal school activities. Just the same, school officials instructed the students to remove the armbands. When they refused, they were sent home and told they were being suspended from school until they returned without their armbands.

Christopher, John, and Mary Beth stayed out of school for about two weeks, returning only after the period previously designated for wearing the armbands had expired. In the meantime, a lawsuit was filed on their behalf in U.S. District Court. The suit asked for an injunction to prevent school officials from disciplining them over the incident or from causing further interference with their right to express their views peaceably in the manner they had chosen.

At a hearing in the federal court, the students testified that they wore the armbands as "a form of witness" against the Vietnam war. They said they hoped their silent demonstration would influence other students to oppose the war. School officials testified they felt the ban was justified on several grounds. They said there were appropriate ways to mourn war dead, but that schools were not the place for such demonstrations. They also feared the wearing of the armbands might create disorder. One official explained that a former student of one of the high schools was killed in Vietnam, and that some of his friends were still in school. If a demonstration took place it might evolve into something which would be difficult to control.

Under questioning by the students' attorneys, school authorities conceded they had made no effort to prohibit the wearing of all symbols of political or controversial significance. The officials testified that students in several schools wore buttons relating to national political campaigns and some even wore the Iron Cross, a traditional symbol of Nazism. Yet, the ban did not cover these—only the black armbands.

After the hearing, the court dismissed the students' suit. It upheld the constitutionality of the school officials' actions on the ground that the Vietnam war was such a controversial issue that the wearing of armbands could logically be assumed to pose a threat to classroom discipline. Therefore, the court said, it was reasonable for the officials to adopt the ban against armbands.

The students' attorneys appealed the federal district court ruling to the Eighth U.S. Circuit Court of Appeals in

St. Louis, Missouri. The appeals court's eight judges divided 4 to 4 on whether to sustain the district court decision. Under the law, such an even split had the effect of upholding the lower court ruling. The case was then appealed to the U.S. Supreme Court.

In a majority opinion written by Justice Abe Fortas (who later resigned from the court), the Supreme Court reversed the rulings of the lower courts. The Supreme Court held decisively that the First Amendment protects the rights of public school children to express their political and social opinions during school hours and that school officials may not place arbitrary curbs on student speech. The decision was considered highly significant because, although civil libertarians had long taken for granted that school children had First Amendment rights of free speech, the Supreme Court had never directly said so prior to this case.

Justice Fortas's opinion said that neither students nor teachers shed their constitutional rights to freedom of speech or expression at the schoolhouse gate. He pointedly referred to the fact that school officials had made no effort to prohibit the wearing of symbolic items other than the black armbands, such as political buttons or Iron Crosses. School officials do not possess absolute authority over their students, the decision said. "Students in school as well as out of school are 'persons' under our Constitution. They are possessed of fundamental rights which the state must respect."

Justice Fortas's majority opinion set off sharp controversy, both on and off the Supreme Court. Justice Hugo Black, who dissented from the majority decision, was among the most outspoken critics. He complained that the decision ushered in a new era in which the "power to control pupils by the elected officials of state-supported public schools in the United States is in ultimate effect transferred to the Supreme Court."

Justice Black's strong dissenting opinion surprised many legal observers, since he had long been a staunch defender of the right of free speech. His views on the Des Moines case, however, were echoed by many who felt the Supreme Court was going too far in the direction of permissiveness toward students. Some, on the other hand, felt Justice Fortas's decision did not go far enough. Among them was David N. Ellenhorn, an American Civil Liberties Union lawyer who had written a brief submitted to the Supreme Court in support of the Des Moines students. Ellenhorn's major complaint was that the Fortas ruling relied heavily on the fact that the Des Moines students' wearing of armbands had caused no serious threat of disruption in the schools. But what if there had been such a threat?

Ellenhorn wrote in the ACLU newspaper, *Civil Liberties.* "Unfortunately, the court's opinion does not say, as it should, whether a student can be stopped from peacefully expressing his views where students of opposing views may react in a disorderly manner."

In spite of these reservations, Ellenhorn saw the decision in the Des Moines case as a major victory that would have widespread repercussions in broadening the rights of students. Before the Supreme Court ruled that the free-speech clause of the Bill of Rights applied to minors, he wrote, many school officials acted as if they had virtually unlimited authority to curb student expression. "Public school students have been forbidden to publish 'underground' newspapers, to organize independent student unions, to criticize the manner in which their schools are run, to engage in leafletting in and around the schools and to take part in many other peaceful forms of expression connected with school. The (Des Moines) case should bury the notion that such limitations can be imposed on student expression and other First Amendment activity. . . . The case leaves many questions unanswered about the exact scope and nature of the student expression which must be permitted under the First Amendment in the classrooms, corridors, and grounds of the public schools. But the case is just the first in what will be a series of challenging and difficult cases defining the rights of our young citizens in their school environment. In holding for the first time that school children are protected by the free-speech clause, the Supreme Court has erected a solid foundation upon which to build."

Ellenhorn's concern with the possibility of school disruption was understandable. Studies of public schools disclosed that an unprecedented wave of school disorders was sweeping the nation. Although student takeovers of buildings on college campuses attracted the lion's share of publicity, the studies disclosed that protests were even more prevalent in high schools than in colleges. And junior highs, to the surprise of many observers, were found to be almost as susceptible to student protests as high schools.

The unrest emerged in every region of the country, disrupting schools in suburbs and rural areas as well as in cities.

In suburban schools, it was found, students had protested against everything from the food in the cafeterias to lack of toilet paper in the rest rooms.

The composition and jurisdiction of student councils were favorite targets of demonstrators. Such councils, which had been considered bold innovations during the 1920s, were now felt to be impotent or the mere tools of school administrators. Further evidence of the disaffection of students was provided by the rapid spread of underground newspapers from college campuses to the high schools and even junior highs. During 1969, the number of underground papers being published by secondary school students increased from about five hundred to one thousand.

Various theories have been advanced on the reasons for the tide of student unrest. B. Frank Brown, director of informational services for I/D/E/A, an educational research organization affiliated with the Charles F. Kettering Foundation, gave this appraisal in a speech to the Education Writers Association: "The current wave of organized high school revolt has its origin in a position paper prepared by a Los Angeles high school student for the Students for a Democratic Society in 1965. This paper, entitled 'High School Reform,' was circulated in mimeographed form for a couple of years and published for wider distribution by the S.D.S. in 1967. The purpose of the position paper was to inform high school students on the best techniques for taking over a high school. Part of the strategy was the establishment of an underground paper."

Many educators, however, saw a much less organized pattern than did Brown. They attributed the protests chiefly to changes in society and the reluctance of teenagers to accept automatically the values of their elders. For example, Alan F. Westin, director of the Center for Research and Education in American Liberties at Columbia University, saw the trend as "a more decentralized and localized kind of thing" than Brown did. "I haven't found any indication of a conspiracy—no blueprint. There is a common pattern, but this is more a cultural phenomenon." Westin pointed out that school disruptions had occurred in such small towns as Edcouch, Texas, population 2,800, as well as large cities and suburbs. A major source of trouble, he said, was that public school systems had been among the last basic institutions to adapt to changes in society.

One school district that did adopt sweeping changes in its policies toward students—at least partially because it had been involved in some of the most violent disorders in the nation—was the New York City public school system. In late 1969, the city board of education issued a policy statement defining the personal and political freedom of high school students, including recognition of the right to peaceful dissent. Among other things, the statement recognized the right of high school students to have a voice in school matters that concern them, generally eliminated censorship of school newspapers, and upheld the right of students to wear buttons, armbands, and "other badges of symbolic expression." It also made clear the right of students to distribute political leaflets and other literature "at locations adjacent to the school" without prior approval of school officials, but provided that advance authority be obtained for distribution of such materials within the school.

Issuance of the policy statement (see Appendix A), which some called a "bill of rights for students," brought mixed reactions. Many student leaders and some school administrators applauded the new provisions, but others criticized them as permissive, restrictive, or vague. John Marson, chairman of the African-American Students Association, which claimed membership in four of New York City's five boroughs, contended the statement was "a racist attempt to deal with the problems of white students but in no way deals with the relevant and legitimate demands of black students." Marson said the statement should have dealt with his association's demands for more black and Puerto Rican teachers and administrators. Walter Degnan, a high school principal and president of the Council of Supervisory Associations (composed of school administrators), criticized the provisions giving students a voice in decisions concerning curriculum and discipline problems. "What if they [students] decide they want three years instead of four years of English or insist on smoking in the schools?" Degnan asked. Others expressed fears that the new guidelines would encourage violent dissent in the schools. These fears prompted the board of education president, Joseph Monserrat, to issue a clarifying statement insisting that student dissent would be tolerated only as long as it was not violent and did not interfere with normal instruction.

Later, student leaders complained that the code still did not go far enough and demanded further concessions. Some legal observers contended the code did not really break much new ground, but rather put into one document a variety of statements on rights that had previously been made by the courts or state education officials. The consensus, however, was that adoption of the code represented a significant step in recognizing student rights and would be used as a model by other school districts across the country.

While the New York board adopted its program only after the city's schools experienced serious violence, it should be noted that some school districts and colleges put similar policies into effect under more placid circumstances. Trinity University in San Antonio, Texas, for example, approved a *Joint Statement on Rights and Free-*

doms of Students, not in response to campus disturbances, but because it felt such action was timely.

Trinity's statement (see Appendix B), issued as a fifteen-page pamphlet, was approved by the university administration, faculty and student government. Since the problems of university and high school students often differ, it is not surprising that the Trinity statement covers some areas ignored in the New York City program.

Trinity's statement described the means by which decisions on disciplinary action would be made and the avenues of appeal open to students. A University Judiciary Board, composed of three faculty members and three students, was empowered to act as a court in ruling on various categories of disciplinary cases. A student court, composed of seven students, was empowered to hear other types of cases. The university president was given power to grant a pardon or clemency in cases decided by either panel, but was not empowered to impose more severe discipline than either group decreed.

Of course, no statement of policy or set of rules is expected to cover all contingencies. The best such a document can hope to do is provide guidelines that may be adapted from time to time to meet changing needs. Moreover, a code adopted in one section of the country may well be unsuited to a school district elsewhere. For, although most students share certain mutual concerns, there often is a wide disparity of priorities from one area to another.

Thus, for example, it would have been highly unlikely for students in a politically conservative region to raise the issue two seventh-graders did recently in liberal-oriented New York City. And it would have been even more unlikely for school administrators in a conservative area to react the way some New York educators did.

The issue the students raised was whether they could be compelled to go through the time-honored ceremony of reciting the Pledge of Allegiance at the beginning of each school day. With the support of their parents, Susan Keller and Mary Frain refused to take part in the recitation at Junior High School 217 in the Jamaica section of Queens, New York. Their principal, Harold Baron, told them they did not have to take part in the actual recitation—but that they must either stand or leave the room while other students were saying the pledge. Again, the two twelve-year-old girls refused. As a protest against the daily recitation, they insisted on remaining seated. Baron suspended them from school.

The girls and their parents explained that they considered the recitation hypocritical. "Liberty and justice for all?" Mary said. "That's not true for the blacks and poor whites. The poor have to live in cold, miserable places. And it's obvious that the blacks are oppressed." Susan's mother, Mrs. Caroline Keller, said her daughter objected to the words "one nation, indivisible, under God," since she did not believe in God. "Nor does she believe in what the pledge says about 'liberty and justice for all,' " Mrs. Keller said. "It's an act of conscience for her to remain seated as a protest, but the school has handled it as an act of insubordination."

The girls' parents filed suit against the school system, seeking not only the students' reinstatement but also a decision barring administrators from compelling any pupils to stand or leave their rooms during the recitation. At a hearing in the case, school officials explained that they had revised their procedures over the years to try to meet changing requirements. From 1953 to 1963, all students were required to recite both the Pledge of Allegiance and the fourth stanza of the hymn *America*—beginning with the words "Our Father's God to thee"—each morning. In addition, during that period, a passage from the Bible was read at all school assemblies.

But in 1963, after the U.S. Supreme Court outlawed compulsory use of the Lord's Prayer or Bible verses in public schools, the New York City board of education discontinued scripture reading at assemblies. It also relaxed the rule calling for the recitation from *America,* substituting for it the singing of any patriotic song. In 1968, the board ruled that students could refrain from reciting the Pledge of Allegiance, but insisted that those who did so must stand or leave the room during recitation. At the hearing in the case of the two suspended students, attorneys for the board argued that such a rule was necessary to prevent disorders from erupting between students who favored the recitation and those who opposed it.

But attorneys for the suspended girls contended that such a procedure violated the girls' constitutional rights. In an affidavit filed with the court, Mary Frain explained her opposition to leaving the room during the recitation. "All the time that I've been in school, being sent out of the room has been associated with punishment," Mary said. She added that she didn't feel "that the actions of this country at this time merit my respect." Her views were echoed in an affidavit from Susan Keller, who said: "I don't want to stand up during the pledge because that is showing respect."

U.S. District Judge Orrin G. Judd, at the conclusion of the hearing, issued a temporary injunction upholding the position taken by the girls. (A temporary injunction is an order barring a defendant in a civil case from taking certain action, pending further court action.) In this case, the injunction barred the board of education from requiring students to stand or leave the room during the recitation of the pledge, and the judge ordered the girls reinstated, directing that they and other students who so desired be permitted to sit at their desks during the pledge.

Dr. Nathan Brown, the acting superintendent of schools, explained that the board of education considered itself caught between two conflicting legal authorities. On one side was Judge Judd's preliminary ruling; on the other was a section of the state education law requiring all school districts to conduct daily patriotic ceremonies.

In compliance with the state law, the board of education had set up its daily program including the Pledge of Allegiance, then had revised the procedure to permit dissenting students to leave the room or stand during the recitation. The question confronting the board after Judge Judd's ruling was whether it could further revise the policy to allow the dissenting students to remain seated and still satisfy the requirements of the state law. In Brown's view, the Judge's decision had called into question the wisdom of requiring any daily ceremony. He asked the State Education Department to consider abolition of the requirement, on the theory that the daily ceremony might lead to more disrespect for the American flag from dissenting students than it would to increased loyalty from others.

While this suggestion was pending, another unexpected development occurred. The New York City High School

Principals Association urged the principals of the city's sixty-three academic high schools, acting on their own authority, to suspend the daily flag ceremony and pledge. The association's executive board, in making the request, said it felt such a suspension was wise in view of the confusion prevailing on the issue. Acceptance of the request by the individual principals would have left 240,000 high school pupils without a daily patriotic ceremony.

The proposal by the association touched off a wave of criticism, particularly from war veterans' organizations. It also brought a prompt decision by the State Education Department, which directed school administrators throughout the state to continue the daily observances and let the courts decide how to deal with dissenters.

Among others critical of the proposal by the principals' association was Mary Frain herself. Just as she insisted on her right to refrain from reciting the pledge, she argued for the rights of other students to continue reciting it. "I think the kids who want to do it ought to be able to do it," Mary said.

Next, the principals' association did an about-face, asking its members to continue requiring the daily ceremonies "for the time being." But indications were that "the time being" would last indefinitely, for the board of education showed no sign it intended to press for a further hearing in the case. Thus, the ceremonies would be continued and those students who objected to the pledge would be permitted to remain seated during the recitation.

To some, the issue seemed trivial. But what was at stake was not alone the rights of two twelve-year-old girls, and those of like minds, to buck the system. What was perhaps more important was the very fact that these two young girls

could succeed in redressing their grievances in legal combat
with such a massive bureaucracy as the New York school
system. Their example was bound to inspire other students,
in New York and elsewhere, to demand recognition of their
rights by school officials. Even before Mary and Susan won
their point, there was ample evidence that students across
the country were moving to secure these rights. Some of
their experiences (which will be discussed in the next chapter) also were considered trivial by their detractors. But, to
those seriously concerned with preserving and broadening
the rights of young Americans, no constitutional issue can
be considered inconsequential.

SUMMARY

*1. The U.S. Supreme Court has held that "students in
school as well as out of school are 'persons' under our constitution . . . (and) possessed of fundamental rights which
the state must respect." Among these rights is freedom to
demonstrate in an orderly fashion within the school, provided no disruptions occur.*

*2. The Supreme Court has not yet ruled on the addi-
tional question of whether such freedom would extend even
if disruptions did occur (for example, disruptions created
by students who opposed the views of the demonstrators).*

*3. School districts and colleges increasingly are adopting
written codes spelling out the rights and responsibilities of
students. The codes generally provide liberalized interpretations of student rights.*

STUDENT RIGHTS: GOVERNMENT, CENSORSHIP, DUE PROCESS

ONE of the most significant developments in the recent trend toward liberalization of young people's rights has been the adoption of the ombudsman concept on behalf of students. An ombudsman is a public official who investigates complaints by citizens against government agencies, then suggests remedies for those complaints he finds justified. The first ombudsman's position was created by the Swedish government in 1810. Similar offices were later created by Denmark, Finland, Norway, New Zealand, and Great Britain. Although the federal government in the United States has not organized an ombudsman's office, several local governments in the United States have done so.

In recent years, largely in response to the wave of disorders sweeping school and college campuses across the country, ombudsmen have been appointed to serve as buffers between students and educators. By early 1970, at least three dozen persons holding the formal title of ombudsmen were functioning on American college campuses. In addition, many others fulfilling similar roles, although not holding the formal title, were operating on both the college and secondary-school levels.

Just what does the educational ombudsman do? The answer varies from one school to another, encompassing everything from mediating between angry students and rigid administrators to handling what appear to be minor gripes.

"I try to help the student who has been caught in the

machinery of the university and snatch him before he becomes completely mangled," says James D. Rust, the ombudsman at Michigan State University. Other campus ombudsmen say they try to serve as "honest brokers" between students and administrators—cutting red tape and trying to bring about changes ranging from elimination of archaic school rules to better treatment of students from minority groups.

The ombudsmen are usually former teachers or administrators, but some are recent graduates. Although they occasionally find themselves caught in the middle of violent confrontations, the majority of their work concerns less dramatic problems—the everyday gripes of average, nonmilitant students. "The ombudsman is for the shy student who is afraid to go and get his just due," says George Gloege, ombudsman at Eastern Montana College. "When agitation comes along, that student is a likely candidate for recruitment to the radicals' cause." By responding to such a student's unvoiced needs, Gloege feels, he may be able to prevent the student from turning to the radicals for solace.

Harry Minor, a former student government president at the University of Detroit, says "the little affronts that build up every day" cause students to lose faith in school administrators. Although the Detroit student government had "never voted unanimously before to do anything except adjourn," Minor says, he persuaded the members to vote unanimously to create an ombudsman's position. Confronted with the unanimous vote, the university administration agreed to establish the job. The man appointed ombudsman at Detroit, Thomas F. Davis, operated chiefly behind the scenes, prodding university officials to act on student complaints without passing the buck. He brought about changes in some teaching assignments based on student complaints, obtained higher grades for students who had been marked unfairly, and got campus employees to fix a slow cafeteria clock that was making students late for classes. Davis drew the line, however, at taking action on one complaint. He decided to ignore the gripe from a student who questioned the need for three rows of cherry yum-yums in an administration building candy machine.

James Rust, the Michigan State ombudsman, says more than one thousand students have come to him with complaints in his two years on the job. About 80 percent of their complaints have been legitimate, he says. Rust describes his job as much like that of a traffic cop, pointing bewildered students in the right direction to get their problems solved. Other than the power of persuasion, he has no formal weapons to compel a teacher or administrator to respond to a student's complaint. But he gets action, he says, "because everyone knows just behind me is standing the (university) president."

Not all campus ombudsmen have even that much authority behind them. Michael Farmer, a student who served as ombudsman at the University of Kentucky, quit his job after two months because "it didn't carry any power." At Cornell University, ombudsman Alice H. Cook concedes her authority is limited. "I have no power to punish, to make decisions, or to institute change," says Mrs. Cook, a sixty-six-year-old mother who brought to her job fourteen years of experience on the campus as a professor of industrial and labor relations. "I investigate complaints, operate as an information center which can function as a rumor clinic during times of crisis, and conduct self-initiated investigations into any aspect of university adminstration." While her power ends there, Mrs. Cook feels, she can still get results because she enjoys the trust of all segments of the campus community.

"Some students, who misunderstand classroom instructions and find they have not fulfilled course requirements, bring their problems to our office," she says. "If there seems to be some real merit to the complaint, we talk to the teacher involved—not to give the student an easy out, but to act as the student's spokesman. Other problems have to do with administration actions and rules—some dealing with student life and dining, lights on the campus at night, rules concerning the campus library." Not surprisingly, since her office was created as a result of a demonstration in which armed black students took control of a campus building, Mrs. Cook spends a good deal of time dealing with militant students. But even more of her time is devoted to the routine complaints of other students. "We seem to see more nonpolitically-minded students who feel their problems are neglected by the administration," she says. "Students are just confused and they have no other place to turn."

Although most ombudsmen restrict themselves to trying to handle each individual student's complaint on a separate basis, they sometimes find so many similar gripes that they move for broad-scale reform of campus rules on such matters as dormitory hours or dating regulations. In some cases, they take on even more ambitious tasks. Nelson F. Norman, the ombudsman at San Diego State College, has lobbied before the California Legislature for increases in the state's student loan program. Ralph Poblano, the ombudsman at San Jose State College, has helped students from minority groups obtain more adequate representation in student government and has visited residents of areas near the college in an effort to combat housing discrimination. In addition, he has aided students in trouble with the law—seeing, for example, that they obtain proper legal counsel.

Besides those official or unofficial ombudsmen operating on school grounds, there are various agencies seeking to perform similar functions off campus. In New York, for example, a Bureau for the Protection of Student Rights has been created by a private organization known as the Metropolitan Applied Research Center. The center is headed by a prominent psychologist and civil rights activist, Dr. Kenneth B. Clark, who is also a member of the State Board of Regents.

Among the primary projects of the Bureau for the Protection of Student Rights is a campaign to protect young people's rights to an education. In particular, the bureau is concerned with students who drop out of school, then wish to return, and those who are expelled for disciplinary reasons. Dr. Clark feels many dropouts and expelled students are unaware of their rights. In New York State, for example, the law requires school districts to provide education for those between the ages of five and twenty-one unless they are high school graduates. The law specifies grounds on which action for a student's removal from the school rolls may be initiated. But Clark maintains that school districts violate the established procedure and illegally expel students without adequate grounds. He points, for example, to the cases of numerous Negro students in New York City who said they stayed home from school for an extended period because they were being harassed by white students. The Negro youngsters were expelled on grounds of truancy. Clark contends the expulsions were in flagrant disregard of the students' rights, since they had stayed home for legitimate reasons, but neither the youngsters nor their parents realized school authorities were acting illegally. The bureau set as one of its first goals the reinstatement of these students. At this writing, their cases have not yet been decided.

Another organization acting to advance student rights was formed in January 1970 at a meeting in Garden City, New York. The organization, known as the Metropolitan Association of Student Governments, is composed of representatives from eleven colleges in the metropolitan New York area. Its aim is to lobby with local, state, and federal governments on issues of interest to students, such as reducing the voting age. An official of the association, Thomas Liotta, says its purpose is to bring about orderly change by working within the framework of the United States Establishment, rather than by trying to topple the Establishment. The colleges represented in the association at its inception were Adelphi, Manhattan, St. John's, Molloy College for Women, the New York Institute of Technology, Nassau Community College, Queens College, Iona, City College, Long Island University, and C. W. Post. Provision was made, however, for representatives of other colleges to join in the future. And the chances seemed strong that other such associations would be formed elsewhere around the country.

One school in the New York area not represented in the association, the State University of New York at Stony Brook, struck out on its own in an unorthodox approach to protecting student rights. The student governing body at Stony Brook, known as Polity, hired an attorney to represent students in their dealings with the administration. The attorney, Richard Lippe, had little trouble understanding the problems of the students since he himself was only a few years out of law school. Lippe, paid a fee of $2,500 from student government funds, was assigned by Polity to investigate the legality of certain administration policies and to "define relationships between administration, faculty, and students."

Among items Lippe was asked to investigate were means of keeping the student government independent (financially and otherwise) of the university administration, protection of students' rights of expression and privacy, and health and safety problems created by construction of numerous new buildings on the campus. Lippe also represented the student body at meetings with university and police officials, aimed at bringing about better police protection on the campus while protecting students against violations of their constitutional rights. Relations with the police became especially sensitive after a series of highly publicized drug raids on the campus, which led to an emotion-charged investigation of the university by a state legislative committee. Students were sharply critical of police tactics, which included use of undercover men posing as students and late-night raids on dormitories. Police officials, in turn, were critical of what they called a lack of cooperation from the administration. Lippe's role in helping bring about agreement among student leaders, police officials, and administration representatives on future policy was praised by all sides.

When university police at Stony Brook began towing away automobiles parked illegally on the campus, the student government asked Lippe to take legal action to prevent further impounding of cars. Lippe filed suit against the university, contending that campus police had no power to impound cars. A judge upheld Lippe's position and issued a restraining order barring the towing away of any additional cars.

Another recent trend promising to expand the rights of young people is the inclusion of students on official bodies that determine school policies. In May 1969 Stephen T. Hughes, president of the student body at the University of Maine, was appointed to the university's board of trustees. He thus became the first student named to a state university board of trustees in the United States. Hughes, a twenty-six-year-old law student, held equal rank with the other fourteen members of the board. Other universities followed suit. In Winston-Salem, North Carolina, Wake Forest University became the first institution in the South to name a student as a trustee. James Estes Cross, the twenty-two-year-old student body president, was given full voting status on the board. New York University, one of the largest private schools in the country, named sixteen students to its chief policy-making body, the university senate. The students made up one-fourth of the senate's membership.

In most cases, the students appointed to the boards were chosen by college administrators. But in Massachusetts Governor Francis W. Sargent went a step farther. He introduced a program giving students in state colleges and universities the right to elect their own representatives on boards of trustees. In a speech describing his plan, Sargent said: "I seek to say to the young student, 'Here will be your chance; here will be your forum. Take it and make it work.'"

There were even rare cases where universities gave students a voice in choosing faculty members. At Harvard University, after two weeks of turmoil in which black students boycotted classes, the Faculty of Arts and Sciences agreed to give them a voice in selecting faculty members for a program in Afro-American studies. The action placed six black students on the thirteen-member Standing Committee on Afro-American Studies, which was given power to exercise general supervision over the program. While there was no stampede by other universities to go so far as Harvard—that is, give students actual voting power on faculty selection—many of them did grant undergraduates an advisory voice in choosing instructors.

On the federal level, the U.S. Office of Education has moved to give students a significant role in shaping government policies that affect campus life. In October 1968 Harold Howe II, who served as U.S. Commissioner of Education during the administration of President Lyndon B. Johnson, directed his aides to call a national conference of student leaders aimed at bringing students into the government decision-making process. In a memorandum issued at the time, Howe suggested that the Office of Education create a youth advisory panel, composed of students, and appoint students to serve on government advisory boards and review panels. In May 1969 fifteen student leaders from various sections of the country, some of them veterans of campus protest movements, met in Washington with top officials of the Office of Education.

The student leaders presented a series of proposals, including the following: (1) Establishment of a permanent Student Advisory Council, reporting directly to the education commissioner, that would propose legislation, offer advice on major education issues and assure continued student participation in government policy-making; (2) appointment of students to one-half of the voting memberships on all advisory committees and task forces determining educational policies; (3) appointment of representative numbers of students to groups reviewing proposals for new educational programs; (4) allocation of government funds to campus projects supported by students; and (5) creation of a system that would permit students to "respond independently" to the Office of Education, instead of being directed to work through their individual school administrators.

Not surprisingly, the proposals were greeted with skepticism and in some cases even hostility by some members of the Office of Education staff. The skeptics pointed out that granting of all the student requests would compel the Office of Education to cast aside guidelines laid down by Congress for operation of the agency. But Dr. James E. Allen, who succeeded Howe as education commissioner shortly after President Richard M. Nixon took office, came to the defense of the student position. "I am very definitely supporting this general move to involve young people here," Allen said. While all details of the student participation have not been ironed out at this writing, it seems clear that young people will be given unprecedented power to influence government decisions affecting education. Allen himself was ousted by the Nixon administration over various policy differences, particularly Allen's views on U.S. military involvement in Southeast Asia.

In a parallel development, students in some states are now being enrolled as full voting members of organizations that have long been targets of their criticism and humor—

the PTAs. Parent-Teacher Associations in Maryland, Florida, and New York have opened their membership rolls to students in response to demands that young people be given more active roles in setting school policies. In most cases, the PTAs involved have changed their names to Parent-Teacher-Student Associations. PTAs in various other states accept students as nonvoting members, and many of them are expected to grant young people voting memberships in the near future.

Such events as the emergence of the ombudsman concept on campus and the granting of decision-making power to students, while encouraging to those who advocate broadening of minors' rights, by no means indicate that students are within sight of their ultimate goals. For one thing, the strides made in some areas of the country in liberalizing student rights have not been made everywhere. For another thing, even in the sections where the greatest advances have been made, most activist students feel at least some of their rights are still being violated.

In New York City, for example, despite the school system's adoption of its policy statement setting out liberalized regulations, militants have continued to protest that students are treated as second-class citizens. To press their demands for further concessions from the board of education, the militants formed a citywide High School Student Union. The tone of their campaign was set in a mimeographed flyer distributed in schools throughout the city, urging students to join the organization:

> As you sit in that drab classroom, as you stare back at the teacher who stares at you from behind his mahogany desk, as you scribble obscenities on your desk

of pine, no doubt you have many times wondered—what the hell am I doing here? You probably think you go to school to learn, to broaden your mind, to understand. The main thing that's taught us in school is how to be good niggers, obey rules, dress in our uniforms, play the game, and NO, Don't be UPPITY! Oh, we're trained for participating in "the democratic process." We have our student governments—they can legislate about basketball games and other such meaningful topics. Don't mention the curriculum—they'll tell us what to learn. Oh, we can express our complaints in the school newspaper—but the principal says what gets printed and don't embarrass the school's reputation.

Spurred by such appeals, thousands of students joined the High School Student Union and continued to press the board of education for additional reforms. The success of the Student Union led, in turn, to formation of other activist student organizations in New York high schools. Negro students organized the Black High School Coalition, which sponsored a boycott of classes by more than two thousand pupils on the anniversary of the assassination of Malcolm X, the black nationalist leader. Opponents of the draft and the Vietnam war won the right to form officially sanctioned school clubs and, in some cases, even to counsel fellow students on how to avoid the draft.

Because of New York's size and its position as the hub of the nation's communications media, events there frequently receive more public notice than comparable occurrences elsewhere. It is perhaps natural, therefore, for some observers to assume that the militance of New York's student activists is a local phenomenon, that students in other cities and towns are less passionate in their demands for greater freedom. Such assumptions, however, seem mistaken. For events of recent years have indicated that students from coast to coast, in both metropolitan and rural areas, are just as committed as New York's militants to the cause of liberalizing young people's rights.

Evidence of this commitment has been provided by demonstrations, boycotts and confrontations in high schools in such disparate geographic areas as Swan Quarter, North Carolina; Boston; Youngstown, Ohio; Sylvester, Georgia; Cedarhurst, Long Island; Milwaukee; Los Angeles; Chicago; and Westport, Connecticut. Although specific issues involved in such protests have varied in detail from community to community, most of them have fallen into a common pattern. For the interests of students in a small rural town are not, after all, much different from those of students in a metropolis.

One frequent source of discontent in schools across the country is administration censorship of student newspapers. For many years, the prevailing view among school administrators was that student newspapers should be bland, uncontroversial publications—echoing the views of the administration, boosting school spirit, and studiously avoiding the making of waves. Since the administrators frequently controlled the newspapers' pursestrings and were able to exert powerful influences on the selection of editors and managers, the staffs of many student papers grudgingly knuckled under to the system.

When the wave of student militancy began sweeping the country, editors of school newspapers were among those demanding freedom from the restrictions of the past. Many

[55]

refused to accept further censorship. They demanded that faculty advisers be removed or, at the very least, be stripped of the authority to censor the views of the editors. In some cases, school administrators recognized that times were changing and moved to grant the newspaper staffs greater freedom than they had enjoyed in the past. But, in other cases, the administrators refused to yield. Their intransigence led to numerous cases in which student editors tried to publish material banned by the educators. Such efforts resulted in the removal of some editors from their newspaper posts, the suspension of the papers themselves, and, in a few cases, even the suspension of the editors from school.

With rare exceptions, disputes over freedom of the student press have been settled—or left unsettled—without resort to lawsuits. One of the exceptions occurred in New York City before the board of education issued its policy statement on student rights, which provided that student newspapers should be generally free from official censorship. Editors of *The Hughes Herald,* the student newspaper at Charles Evans Hughes High School, wrote an editorial criticizing what they considered the prevailing attitudes among the school's teachers and administrators. They showed the article to their faculty adviser, who approved its publication. But, before the paper went to press, Principal Samuel Namowitz heard about the editorial and asked to read it.

When given a copy of the editorial, Namowitz objected strenuously to its content and ordered it deleted from the paper. The staff complied, publishing a bland substitute in place of the original. At the same time, however, a half-dozen staff members printed handbills containing the censored editorial and an account of Namowitz's actions. They distributed the handbills on the streets outside the school. Namowitz then called in the *Herald's* editor-in-chief, Peter Hodes, and told him he would have to resign his position on the paper. Namowitz contended that Hodes could not continue to be editor of the paper while assailing school policies in handbills. Hodes, who had been one of the two authors of the original editorial, argued that his dual role provided no conflict of interests. He contended that, in distributing the handbills, he was merely exercising his constitutional rights as a citizen. But Namowitz refused to budge; he insisted Hodes would have to resign. Hodes declined to do so, and was told by Namowitz that he was being fired as editor. His ouster was followed by the resignations of most members of the newspaper staff and by the firing of the faculty adviser who had approved the editorial's publication.

Hodes took his case to the American Civil Liberties Union, which filed suit seeking his reinstatement as editor. The ACLU contended in the suit that Namowitz had violated Hodes's constitutional rights by punishing him for distributing the handbills outside the school. The board of education did not fight the case, so Hodes was awarded his desired court order by default. The order directed school authorities to reinstate him as editor. The ruling, however, concerned only the question of Hodes's right to distribute the handbills. It did not go into the larger matter of school administrators' authority to censor student publications. At this writing, no court has decided a case involving the right of the student press to remain free of official censorship. As a result, many student editors continue to be subject to restrictions placed on them by teachers and administrators.

Because of such restrictions, large numbers of student journalists have abandoned the notion of publishing controversial material in official school papers and turned instead to the publication of underground newspapers outside the control of school authorities. In some cases, the readership of the underground papers far exceeds that of the official publications. The material published in the underground papers—including radical political articles, explicit discussions of sexual matters, coverage of the drug scene, and frequent use of obscene language—is a far cry from the content of the typical school paper.

Publishing such papers outside the school does not necessarily free staff members from attempted harassment by school officials and other authorities. In a recent case in Delaware, for example, two high school students were arrested on charges of blasphemy and lewdness because of material published in their underground paper. They were the first persons charged with violation of the state's blasphemy law in more than half a century. The students, Matthew Alan Bennett, seventeen, and William F. Bertolette, eighteen, were copublishers of a paper called *The Acid Flash,* distributed primarily among their fellow students at Mount Pleasant High School.

The blasphemy charge against them was based on an article in the paper entitled *The Purple Jesus, or the Grape of the Virgin,* which used the word bastard in referring to Christ. The lewdness charge was based on another article in the paper, which purported to be a review of a motion picture about morbid sex acts. In addition to facing the criminal charges, Bennett was suspended from school for selling copies of the newspaper inside the school. At this writing, the criminal cases have not yet come to trial and there is some question whether they ever will. The constitutionality of the laws involved have been questioned, leading Delaware prosecutors to doubt the wisdom of pressing the charges. Nonetheless, the very fact that the two students were arrested underscores the hazards involved in publishing an underground paper that dares to defy the conventions of society.

Such hazards were made strikingly clear to the editor of an underground paper published by a group of students attending Louis D. Brandeis High School in New York City. The paper published an article containing the following passage: "We must wipe out this school of death. We must wipe out these teachers of death, we must wipe out this education of death. We're gonna get them. We are going to rise up and take them in our fists and throw them to the dogs and rats. We are going to send the pigs back to the farm."

Although the paper was published outside the school and had no official sanction, it naturally stirred considerable antagonism among teachers and administrators. When the editor was found distributing copies in the school lunchroom, he was suspended. The editor took the case to court, charging that the suspension violated his constitutional rights to due process, free speech, and freedom of the press. His case has not yet been decided. But, when it is, the ruling is likely to prove highly significant for staffs of numerous other underground papers. For the chief legal issue arising from publication of underground papers appears to be whether school administrators may ban their distribution within the school grounds.

The American Civil Liberties Union, in an attempt to cut through the legal fog surrounding attempts to censor both official and underground student publications, has issued a set of suggested guidelines on freedom of the student press. The guidelines are contained in a pamphlet covering the entire subject of academic freedom in secondary schools (see Appendix C).

Of course, the guidelines proposed by the ACLU represent an ideal situation from the viewpoint of the student journalist and civil libertarian. In practice, very few school administrators are yet willing to subscribe to such suggestions. But, by referring to the guidelines, student reporters and editors may gauge the comparative freedoms they enjoy and evaluate the areas in which they may reasonably expect to win expansion of their rights.

The ACLU has also issued a set of proposed guidelines on another issue of primary importance to students—the right of due process (see Appendix D). Put simply, the right of due process refers to the student's right to be treated fairly—under an established, orderly system—when subjected to discipline by school authorities. In all too many cases, the ACLU feels, students are arbitrarily deprived of the right of due process. Ira Glasser, associate director of the New York Civil Liberties Union, put it this way in a memorandum to some of his colleagues: "It is startling to note that there is almost no due process for students and that, as a result, grave injustices and gross abuses of fairness take place. To a great extent, whatever procedures do exist serve mainly to legitimize whatever decision has been taken [by school administrators]. A school system which does not treat its students fairly cannot expect to teach or instill respect for due process."

The guidelines drawn up by the ACLU aim to fill the void described by Glasser.

As in the case of the guidelines on the student press, the ACLU guidelines on due process go far beyond the procedures now in effect in most schools. Such guidelines may take decades to win general acceptance, if indeed they ever win acceptance. But, again, they provide students with a useful yardstick and set of possible goals.

SUMMARY

1. Ombudsmen and other buffers between students and educators are helping young people win recognition of their rights in an orderly, responsible fashion.

2. Increased militancy by students is creating broad new associations, whose reach goes far beyond the traditional student councils, aimed at lobbying and organizing on behalf of student rights. Such associations are stretching their influence across school district and state lines, and undoubtedly will lead to even wider participation on a national basis.

3. Despite resistance from some administrators, underground newspapers are gaining acceptance in many schools. The courts are likely to uphold freedom of the underground press and recognized student publications, within limits that vary from jurisdiction to jurisdiction. But a key issue—whether underground papers may be distributed on school grounds in defiance of administrators' wishes—has not yet been decided by the courts.

4. Students in some districts still do not have clear rights to due process of law in such matters as hearings on disciplinary action, but they are likely to gain such rights in the future. This area probably will be one in which civil libertarians will be most active in the coming months and years.

EMPLOYMENT, DRIVING, CONTRACTS AND LEGAL AGREEMENTS, MONEY, VOTING

OUTSIDE the school, some of the most bewildering questions confronting the person under twenty-one concern his rights in the business world. These involve such subjects as the exercise of his rights when holding a job, entering into a legal agreement (for example, a contract to buy an automobile), or trying to control his own finances.

The minor who seeks a job for the first time often finds a seemingly impenetrable jungle of red tape in his path —forms to fill out, restrictions to heed, obstacles to hurdle. But these apparent roadblocks are actually not so formidable as they appear at first glance, and most of them exist chiefly for the protection of the young person.

Since the late nineteenth century, child labor laws have been in effect in the United States. Under these laws, most states forbid children under fourteen to work in factories and almost half the states forbid children under sixteen to work during school hours. In addition, various laws protect young people from working excessively long hours, performing work beyond their physical capacities, or operating dangerous machines.

In many states, persons under eighteen must obtain working papers before taking jobs. Most schools in such states provide application forms and information about working papers to interested students. To obtain working papers, a minor usually is required to get written permission from his parent or guardian. He then takes to his prospective employer a certificate in which the employer pledges to hire the youngster, describes the kind of work to be done and the work schedule. The minor must pass a physical examination and provide legal proof of age, such as a birth certificate or a certificate of age issued by his school district.

For those younger than sixteen, state laws generally restrict job opportunities to lighter types of work than those available to older teenagers. A farm worker younger than sixteen may be required to obtain a farm work permit. In some areas, before a teenager may drop out of school to take a job, he must attend a school work-orientation program or register for evening courses.

Regardless of age, almost anyone holding a job must have a social security card. Those applying for work for the first time may obtain social security cards from the nearest office of the U.S. Social Security Administration. They will find when they receive their paychecks that some of their earnings have been withheld for payment into the government's Social Security fund. Such payments provide a form of insurance against major economic hazards. Those holding social security cards, and their dependents, become eligible for insurance benefits intended to replace at least partially earnings lost through old age, disability, or deaths in their families.

Some occupations, especially those involving manual crafts and trades, require new employees to enter apprenticeship programs that may last several years. An employer hiring a young person to work in an apprenticeship program signs a contract pledging to provide specified training. Sometimes, apprenticeship programs are administered by labor unions. In either case, the young person's right to get the promised training is protected by state and federal laws. Any apprentice who feels his employer or labor union is failing to meet the terms of his apprenticeship contract may file a complaint with the U.S. Labor Department and/or the appropriate state agency.

Even in cases where young workers are not involved in apprenticeship programs, they may be required to join labor unions. Some contracts between unions and employers provide that all workers must join the unions after stated periods of employment. In cases where such contracts are not in force, the young employee may want to join the union anyway. Labor unions exist, in theory at least, to protect the rights of the workers and bargain on their behalf. They are subject to regulation by the state and federal governments, for the protection of members, employers, and the public at large. A union member who has evidence of corruption or malfeasance by one or more of his labor leaders may file a complaint with the Labor Department, the state, or a local prosecuting attorney. Similarly, complaints may also be filed against employers who resort to unfair labor practices in dealing with their workers.

A person under twenty-one is entitled to the same minimum-wage guarantees as an adult under present law. The minimum wage established by federal law is $1.60 an hour. Some states have their own laws, with minimums varying according to industry and occupation. Numerous jobs held by young people—such as those of delivery boys, porters, and clerks in very small businesses—are exempt from the federal law. But most jobs in large establishments whose business transactions involve some sort of interstate commerce are included. Employers are forbidden to discriminate in pay scales between boys and girls working at identical jobs. They are, of course, permitted to establish higher wage scales for experienced, skilled workers than for beginning, unskilled employees.

In late 1969 U.S. Secretary of Commerce Maurice H. Stans disclosed that the Nixon administration was considering legislation to reduce the minimum wage for persons under twenty-one from the present $1.60 an hour to $1.20 or $1.25. Stans said such legislation would help reduce unemployment among young people, who have the highest jobless rate in the country. "After they reach twenty-one, they would receive the regular mimimum wage," he said. "I think that would be a very effective means of reducing unemployment and bringing them into the work force." Despite Stans's assessment, the proposal stirred criticism among young people and some labor leaders. At this writing, the Nixon administration has not yet announced whether it will press for passage of the legislation.

Closely allied to the young person's rights in the employment field are his rights in relation to driving a motor vehicle, since many jobs require the employee to drive while at work or in reaching his employer's place of business. State laws vary considerably on such matters as minimum ages for drivers, hours during which young people may drive and special conditions that must be met. (A detailed, state-by-state analysis of driving regulations applying to young people will be found in Appendix E to this book.) Here is a brief summary of the regulations establishing minimum ages for driving automobiles.

The nation's youngest legal drivers are in Montana, which permits thirteen-year-olds to drive in hardship cases such as the absence of other available transportation to and from school. Fourteen-year-olds are allowed to drive, provided certain criteria are met, in Alaska, Arkansas, Idaho, Iowa, Kansas, New Mexico, North Dakota, South Dakota, and Wisconsin. Fifteen-year-olds may drive in Alabama, Florida, Georgia, Hawaii, Illinois, Indiana, Louisiana, Maine, Minnesota, Mississippi, Missouri, Nebraska, New Hampshire, Oregon, South Carolina, Texas, Vermont, Washington state, and Wyoming.

California, Nevada, North Carolina, and Oklahoma permit driving at the age of fifteen and a half, Arizona at fifteen years and seven months, Virginia at fifteen years and eight months, and Colorado at fifteen years and nine months. Sixteen-year-olds may drive in Connecticut, Delaware, Kentucky, Maryland, Massachusetts, Michigan, New York, Ohio, Pennsylvania, Rhode Island, Tennessee, Utah, West Virginia, and the District of Columbia. In New Jersey, there is a minimum driving age of seventeen.

Almost half the states require special examinations and licenses for the operation of motorcycles and motor scooters. Some of them permit operation of such vehicles, particularly motor scooters, at a younger age than they allow driving of an automobile. About half the states impose the same requirements for motorcycles and motor scooters as they do for automobiles. (Details on regulations covering motorcycles and motor scooters will be found in the appendix.)

In some states, special restrictions are imposed on drivers younger than twenty-one, in addition to the limitations on on the hours when they may drive. For example, in New York State, more stringent rules are applied to drivers under twenty-one than to adults in enforcement of the drunk-driving laws. In order to convict an adult of driving while his ability is impaired by alcohol, the prosecution must prove that a chemical test shows at least ten-hundredths of 1 percent of alcohol in his blood. For those under twenty-one, a conviction is possible if the test shows only five-hundredths of 1 percent of alcohol. In addition, New York has a law forbidding anyone to drive a truck more than five miles while more than five persons under eighteen are riding in the truck body, unless at least one person over twenty-one also rides in the body.

A young person with a job and a driver's license often assumes that, as soon as he saves enough money for the down payment or full purchase price, he can go out and buy a car. It's not necessarily so. He may need to have his parent or guardian sign the purchase contract and other legal papers, since most states do not consider binding any contracts signed by minors. Moreover, merchants tend to be wary of dealing directly with minors, particularly on installment-plan purchases. Thus, a person under twenty-one may find that, although his money is being spent, he doesn't get official ownership of the car or other item being bought. The registration papers, ownership, and responsibility all must be placed in his parent's name.

A recent court case in Riverhead, Long Island, underscored the legal hazards involved for anyone who tries to enforce a contract with a minor. A nineteen-year-old college student, David Silva, attended a sale on repossessed automobiles conducted by the Suffolk County Sheriff's office. Silva bought a 1968 Chevrolet at the sale for $1,100. Three days later he was informed that General Motors Acceptance Corporation, which had financed the sale of the car to the previous owner, held a $2,400 lien against the automobile. Sheriff Frank Gross notified Silva that he would have to pay an additional $1,300 in order to satisfy the lien. Silva retained a lawyer, David Gilmartin, who filed suit to have the sale declared void. Gilmartin contended in court that Silva, although nineteen, had the same legal rights as an infant and could not be a party to a valid contract. State Supreme Court Justice William R. Geiler upheld this argument and declared the contract invalid. He ordered the sheriff to return Silva's $1,100 and to turn the car over to General Motors Acceptance Corporation.

Assuming a young person succeeds in gaining use of an automobile—by having his parent buy it on his behalf or some other means—he may find difficulties in insuring the car that do not normally confront adults. Some insurance companies are reluctant to insure cars that are driven principally by young people. In addition, insurance rates for young drivers frequently are higher than those for adults. These circumstances, however, do not represent deliberate discrimination by the insurance companies. Insurance rates are based on past performance records, and statistics indicate that young drivers are involved in proportionately more accidents than their elders, thus causing the insurance companies to make more payment claims *per capita* than adults. The companies feel, therefore, that it is only fair to charge increased rates for young drivers.

Of course, there are many business matters having nothing to do with automobiles in which a minor finds his age becomes a complication. The recent upsurge in the number of young people entering the entertainment business —for example, as musicians or members of singing groups —provides a case in point. It is often necessary for such entertainers to enter into contracts involving club dates, recording agreements, and the like. Just as in the case of an automobile purchase agreement, a contract of this kind usually is not considered binding if signed by a minor alone on his own behalf. The signature of a parent or guardian may be required to validate the contract. Many inexperienced performers who have not yet reached twenty-one eagerly sign any contract offered them, ignorant of the fact that the agreement may be invalid. Some find later that such agreements can easily be broken by other parties, who are confident the courts will not compel them to meet the terms of contracts involving minors.

Other problems confronting persons under twenty-one involve their rights to use their own money as they please. They do not always enjoy the same rights as adults. For instance, a minor who inherits money is not free to spend it any way he chooses. The probate judge in charge of settling the estate usually appoints a guardian, often one of the minor's parents, to oversee the management of the money. The guardian, however, may not spend any of the money without satisfying the judge that the expenditure is necessary for the minor's welfare. When the minor turns twenty-one, he gains full control of the funds.

The minor who holds a job and resides with his parents may face other puzzling questions concerning money, questions for which there are no firm legal answers. For example, must he share with his parents the money he earns? Must he contribute toward the family's rent or mortgage payment, food, clothing, and other costs? If he is a college student, holding a part-time job, must he pay part or all of his education costs? The courts have not decisively settled any of these questions, as such, but have generally held that parents are responsible for supporting their children until adulthood is reached. Such rulings, however, have not been intended to grant minors licenses to behave as freeloaders when they are earning reasonably substantial salaries. In the final analysis, questions of this nature must be settled through good-faith discussions between young people and their parents. Judges have taken the position that these are problems to be solved within the family, not within the courtroom. (Other matters involving a young person's rights in relation to his parents will be discussed in a later chapter.)

Closely allied to rights in the business world and to various other vital concerns of young people is the right to vote. Many minors argue that, if they are to assume responsible positions in society and try to eliminate some of the discrimination practiced against them, they must have their say at the polls. Although influential voices recently have been heard advocating a reduction in the voting age, minors currently are allowed to vote in only four states. In Georgia and Kentucky (plus the United States territory of Guam), the voting age is eighteen. In Alaska, it is nineteen; in Hawaii, twenty. All other states require voters to be twenty-one. Recent attempts to lower the voting age in New Jersey, Ohio, and Nebraska have been defeated at the polls, but similar proposals are pending in twelve other states.

Among the twelve is New York, where Governor Nelson A. Rockefeller proposed late in 1969 that eighteen-year-olds be given the franchise. In New York State, he said, there are nearly a million young people between eighteen and twenty-one, of whom 67 percent have been graduated from high school, more than 50 percent are employed and pay taxes, nearly 20 percent are married and have assumed family responsibilities, and nearly seventy thousand under twenty-one are serving with the armed forces.

The New York proposal illustrates the difficulties involved in changing state voting laws. In order for Rockefeller's proposal to take effect, it would have to be passed at two consecutive sessions of the state legislature and then approved by the state's voters. Similar, though not identical, obstacles confront those trying to bring about reduced voting ages in other states.

On the national level, the issues were clouded when Congress passed a law in 1970 giving eighteen-year-olds the right to vote in all elections. President Nixon, though he had grave doubts about the law's constitutionality, signed it—thus setting the stage for a possibly lengthy court test. The President's reservations were based on the manner in which Congress put through the legislation. Initially, it was thought that a constitutional amendment would be necessary to accomplish the purpose of granting the ballot to eighteen-year-olds. The law that was passed, however, made no provision for a constitutional amendment; it simply purported to grant the vote to the young people. Whether the law will be upheld by the courts is another question, which must await the tests of time. In the congressional hearings leading up to passage of the controversial law, numerous issues of importance to young people's rights were raised. The Nixon administration, for example, pointedly refrained from supporting various measures intended to grant across-the-board voting rights in all elections to eighteen-year-olds. Instead, it backed a proposal granting the franchise only in elections for President, Vice President, senator and congressman.

The administration's position was spelled out by Deputy Attorney General Richard G. Kleindienst in testimony before a Senate subcommittee considering the proposed amendment. Kleindienst pointed out that Great Britain, which originated the traditional voting age of twenty-one, recently changed its law to give eighteen-year-olds the ballot. Kleindienst said that if we have sufficient confidence in young people to permit them to assume military, employment, and tax responsibilities, we should not keep them on the sidelines as far as the right to vote is concerned.

Answering the contentions of those who oppose lowering the voting age on the ground that young people have showed irresponsibility by participating in violent demonstrations, Kleindienst offered three counterarguments: First, that many persons involved in such demonstrations are past the age of twenty-one; second, that those who have engaged in disturbances represent only a small percentage of young Americans; and, third, that giving youths a role in the political process may eliminate the sense of frustration and feeling of noninvolvement that possibly have contributed to the irresponsible behavior of some young people. "The ballot box is the best place to channel the opinions of such people—within, not without, the existing political framework," Kleindienst testified.

The Senate subcommittee heard testimony from numerous other witnesses supporting the proposed amendment. Theodore C. Sorensen, a former aide to Presidents John F. Kennedy and Lyndon B. Johnson, bore down heavily in his testimony on the fact that many of the American soldiers fighting in Vietnam were not old enough to vote. Sorensen and other witnesses blamed news media coverage of campus disturbances in part for the reluctance of many states to grant eighteen-year-olds the vote.

Sorensen's testimony was supported by Dr. S. I. Hayakawa, president of San Francisco State University, who gained national attention for his hard-line approach to disturbances on his campus. Of the 18,000 students at San Francisco State, Hayakawa testified, no more than 1,000 participated actively in the disruptions. Of the 700 arrested during the demonstrations, he said, only half were students and their average age was twenty-three. Their leaders were twenty-four to thirty, he said. But when he tried to interest television stations and networks in covering some constructive activities of the remaining 17,000 students, he said, there wasn't a single response.

Senator Jennings Randolph of West Virginia, the sponsor of a proposed constitutional amendment on the subject, testified that lowering the voting age was necessary to expand the base of our democracy. He said federal action was needed because the process of waiting for each state to change its individual voting law would be too slow to meet the needs of our changing society.

The surge of activity on behalf of granting the franchise to eighteen-year-olds provides additional evidence of the national trend toward broadening the rights of young people. No matter what the outcome, it seems clear that the general trend will continue and accelerate in the coming years.

SUMMARY

1. Young people who hold jobs are entitled to the same minimum pay as adults, but their wages beyond the minimum may be limited because of lack of experience, etc.

Girls are entitled to the same pay scales as boys, under federal law, provided they perform similar work.

2. Minors generally are not considered legally bound by contracts they may sign, unless their parents or guardians also sign.

3. Minors who inherit money usually may not spend it as they choose, but their parents or guardians must manage the money in the best interests of the young persons. Once a minor reaches twenty-one, he almost always gains control of his funds.

4. The clear trend is toward giving minors the right to vote before they reach twenty-one. At this writing, it is not yet clear how soon national voting ages will be reduced. But the day when eighteen-year-olds are allowed to vote nationwide is not far off.

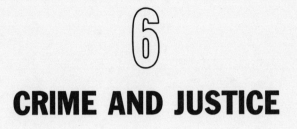

6

CRIME AND JUSTICE

ONE field in which the rights of young people are violated perhaps more than any other is criminal law. Rights that would ordinarily be honored in the case of an adult accused of a crime are routinely and systematically ignored in the cases of many juveniles charged with delinquency. Some authorities argue that different systems of justice are necessary in the handling of adult and juvenile criminals, since the methods of punishment and rehabilitation theoretically differ sharply between the two groups. Others contend that juvenile delinquents are already being "coddled" by the courts and that liberalization of their rights would lead to further acceleration of the spiraling rate of juvenile crime.

There can be no disputing the fact that crimes committed by minors are increasing at an alarming rate. Between 1960 and 1965, the latest period for which complete records are available, there was a 52-percent rise in the number of arrests of persons under eighteen for such crimes as willful homicide, rape, robbery, aggravated assault, larceny, burglary, and auto theft. During the same period, arrests of persons over eighteen for these same crimes increased only 20 percent. The President's Commission on Law Enforcement and Administration of Justice reported that "enormous numbers of young people" appear to be involved in delinquent acts.

Just what is a juvenile court? How does it function? How does its operation differ from a court in which adults are tried? And how well has the juvenile-court system worked?

Basically, juvenile courts are judicial tribunals that deal in special ways with young people's cases. The cases they handle include delinquency—violations of the criminal codes, truancy, general ungovernability, and certain conduct illegal only for children—and such other matters as parental neglect. The juveniles under such courts' jurisdiction are those below a designated age, which ranges in various states from sixteen to twenty-one. Court authority over the youth involved generally ends when he reaches twenty-one. Juvenile courts differ from adult criminal courts in several major respects, reflecting the theory that errant minors should be protected and rehabilitated, rather than subjected to the harshness of the criminal-court system.

In place of the adversary system of justice, which pits prosecution against defense in a battle of evidence, the juvenile courts employ much less formal procedures. The judge acts both as a fact finder and an arbiter. Often, the juvenile is not represented by a lawyer. His fate is generally in the hands of the judge alone, rather than a judge and jury. Emphasis is placed on investigation of the juvenile's background, to a greater degree than in the adult criminal courts, in deciding the disposition of his case. Judges sometimes rely heavily on social scientists, in addition to law-enforcement officers, for advice on diagnosis of the juvenile's problems and methods of bringing about his rehabilitation.

The informal procedures employed by juvenile courts, while theoretically designed for the benefit of the young people involved, often lead to abuses of their rights. Moreover, there is ample evidence that such courts are falling far short of achieving their stated objectives. As the President's Commission on Law Enforcement and Administration of Justice put it: "The great hopes originally held for the juvenile court have not been fulfilled."

Various reasons were given by the commission for the failure of juvenile courts. One was the unwillingness of most American communities to provide the resources—people, funds, facilities, and concern—necessary to permit such courts to realize their potential. More than four-fifths of the juvenile judges polled in a recent survey reported they had no psychiatrist or psychologist available to their courts on a regular basis, the commission reported. Even more important, the commission noted, is the low caliber of many juvenile court judges.

"One crucial presupposition of the juvenile court philosophy—a mature and sophisticated judge, wise and well versed in law and the science of human behavior—has proved in fact too often unattainable," the commission said. "A recent study of juvenile court judges in the United States revealed that half had no undergraduate degree; a fifth had received no college education at all; a fifth were not members of the bar. Almost three-quarters devote less than a quarter of their time to juvenile and family matters, and judicial hearings often turn out to be little more than . . . interviews of ten to fifteen minutes' duration."

Under such circumstances, it is easy to see how the rights of young people might frequently be violated in juvenile court proceedings. For years, many of these violations went unchallenged. But in recent years, with the growing trend toward liberalization of minors' rights, juvenile court procedures have come under increasingly sharp legal attacks.

[83]

Various appellate court decisions have ordered the juvenile courts to make available to young people rights comparable to those accorded adults. Of these, probably the most significant decision was issued by the U.S. Supreme Court in the case of a juvenile named Gerald Francis Gault.

Gerald, then fifteen, was first adjudged a juvenile delinquent by a judge in Gila County, Arizona, on February 25, 1964. He was placed on six months' probation for being in the company of another boy who stole a wallet from a woman's purse. On June 8, 1964, while Gerald was still on probation, one of his woman neighbors made a verbal complaint to sheriff's officers accusing him of telephoning her and using obscene language. On the basis of the verbal complaint, and without a warrant or court order, officers arrested Gerald that same day.

His mother and father, Marjorie and Paul Gault, were both at work at the time of his arrest. No notice that he had been taken into custody was left at the home and no other steps were taken to advise the Gaults of the arrest. When Mrs. Gault arrived home from work, she became puzzled by Gerald's absence and sent another son to look for him. Gerald's brother went to the home of a friend, who knew about the arrest, and only then learned that Gerald was in custody. The brother and Mrs. Gault went to the Gila County Detention Home, where a probation officer told them "why Gerry was there" and told them that a juvenile court hearing would be conducted at three o'clock the next afternoon.

No formal complaint was filed in the case until Gerald had been in custody for a full day. Then, shortly before the hearing in his case, the probation officer filed a petition (legal request) with the court. The petition asked for a hearing and an order concerning "the care and custody" of the youth. The petition was not served on the Gaults, and they did not even see it until more than two months later. Even if they had, it would have given them little information on which to base a defense. It said merely that Gerald was considered a delinquent minor in need of the court's protection.

At the time set for the hearing Gerald, his mother, his older brother, and two probation officers appeared before the juvenile court judge in his chambers. Gerald's father could not attend because he was working out of town. The woman who had made the verbal complaint was not present. No witnesses were sworn, no transcript or recording of the proceedings was made, and no memorandum of the substance of the hearing was prepared. As a result, there were later conflicts among the participants on just what had occurred at the hearing.

Gerald's mother, for example, recalled that her son, when questioned by the judge about the lewd telephone call, said he had merely dialed the neighbor's number and then handed the phone to a friend, Ronald Lewis. Her recollection was that Gerald said the purportedly obscene remarks had been made by Ronald. But one of the probation officers contended Gerald had admitted making the remarks. The juvenile court judge supported the probation officer, saying he recalled that Gerald had "admitted making one of these (lewd) statements." At the conclusion of the hearing, the judge said he would "think about" the case before making a decision.

In the meantime, Gerald was taken back to the detention home. Three days later, without explanation, he was released and driven home. A probation officer gave Mrs.

Gault a note informing her that a further hearing would be conducted on June 15. At the second hearing, conditions were similar to those at the first—no record was made, no witnesses were sworn, no memorandum was prepared. And, once again, the woman who had made the verbal complaint was not present. Not surprisingly, some of those present again differed on what happened at the hearing.

Mr. and Mrs. Gault (the father was present at the second hearing) later recalled that Gerald again testified he had only dialed the neighbor's number and that Ronald had made the lewd remarks. A probation officer agreed that, at this hearing, Gerald denied making the remarks. But the judge claimed "there was some admission again of some of the lewd statements, [although] he didn't admit any of the more serious lewd statements." Mrs. Gault complained at the second hearing about the neighbor's absence, saying she thought the woman should be present. But the judged ruled that the woman didn't have to be present. The judge had never spoken to the woman and a probation officer had talked to her only once, by telephone.

When the second hearing ended, the judge committed Gerald as a juvenile delinquent to the State Industrial School "for the period of his minority [that is, until he reached twenty-one] unless sooner discharged by due process of law." In his written order placing Gerald in the custody of the state school, the judge wrote that "said minor is a delinquent child and that said minor is of the age of fifteen years."

Arizona law does not permit an appeal of a decision by a juvenile court judge, but Gerald's parents were determined to fight the commitment order against him. They retained attorneys who filed a petition for a writ of habeas

[86]

corpus, seeking his release. A writ of habeas corpus is an order requiring that a prisoner be brought to court, usually to determine whether he is being wrongfully imprisoned. The lawyers' petition was referred to the Arizona Superior Court for a hearing.

At the hearing, the juvenile court judge was cross-examined vigorously on the basis for his commitment order. He testified that he had taken into account the fact that Gerald was already on probation when arrested in the telephone-call case. His testimony disclosed that the law Gerald was accused of violating provided that a person who, "in the presence of or hearing of any woman or child . . . uses vulgar, abusive, or obscene language, is guilty of a misdemeanor." The penalty provided under state law for this misdemeanor, if committed by an adult, was a fine of $5 to $50 or jailing for not more than two months. Yet, for the same alleged offense, Gerald faced possible incarceration at the state school for as long as six years.

The juvenile court judge also testified that his decision had been based in part on an Arizona law defining a juvenile delinquent as one who is "habitually involved in immoral matters." Asked to support his contention that Gerald had been "habitually involved in immoral matters," the judge said he vaguely recalled an incident two years earlier in which Gerald was supposed to have stolen a baseball glove from another boy and lied to the police department about it. He conceded that there had been no formal accusation or hearing related to that incident "because of lack of material foundation." But the event remained in his memory and, by his own description, entered into his decision to commit Gerald.

Despite this testimony, the Superior Court refused to grant the writ of habeas corpus sought by Gerald's lawyers.

The attorneys then carried the case to the Arizona Supreme Court, which also denied the writ. Ultimately, the case was taken to the U.S. Supreme Court. Gerald's attorneys asked the high court to order his release and to rule that the juvenile court laws of Arizona were invalid. They maintained that the state laws violated the due-process clause of the Fourteenth Amendment by permitting a juvenile to be taken from the custody of his parents and committed to a state institution through proceedings in which the juvenile court had virtually unlimited powers. Specifically, they charged that the juvenile court judge and the Arizona laws had violated Gerald's constitutional rights by failing to give him and his parents adequate notice of the charges against him; by failing to see that he was represented by an attorney in the original hearings; by denying him the opportunity to confront and cross-examine the woman complainant and other witnesses; by denying him the privilege to avoid testifying against himself; by failing to provide a transcript of the hearings; and by failing to provide a means under which the juvenile court's decision could be directly appealed.

After receiving written briefs and hearing oral arguments in the case, the Supreme Court issued its decision on May 15, 1967—almost three years after Gerald's arrest. The court's majority opinion was written by Justice Abe Fortas.

"Under our Constitution, the condition of being a boy does not justify a kangaroo court," Fortas wrote. While he did not specifically accuse the Arizona court of being a kangaroo court, he made clear that many of the basic rights that would have been granted an adult had been denied Gerald. For example, he would have been guaranteed the right to counsel (and, if necessary, court-appointed attorneys would have represented him without charge), the right to confront and cross-examine witnesses, protection against illegal arrest, search, seizure, or questioning. Virtually all these rights had been violated in Gerald's case, Fortas wrote. "So wide a gulf between the state's treatment of the adult and of the child requires a bridge sturdier than mere verbiage," he said.

The Supreme Court, for these reasons, reversed the previous court orders and directed that Gerald be released. The decision promised far-reaching impact—not only in the juvenile courts but in other fields as well. Among the most significant passages of the ruling was one clause saying simply that "neither the Fourteenth Amendment nor the Bill of Rights is for adults alone." If applied across the board, in all sorts of circumstances involving minors, that clause could remedy many of the forms of discrimination practiced against those under twenty-one.

But that "if" is a big one. In order for a Supreme Court decision to have sweeping effect, it goes without saying that it must be heeded by the judges in subsequent lower court proceedings. In the case of the Gault decision, many juvenile court judges throughout the country have revised their procedures to meet the standards imposed by the Supreme Court. And the very existence of the Gault decision has made some young people, parents, and their lawyers aware of the rights that should be respected by juvenile courts. But the fact remains that numerous juvenile court judges are either unfamiliar with the Gault decision or have chosen to disregard it. Thus, in order to exercise the rights the Supreme Court has ruled are theirs, many young people must go through the time-consuming, often costly process of appealing the original rulings issued by juvenile courts.

In 1969, two years after the Gault decision was handed down, the *Christian Science Monitor,* in a series of articles written by Howard James, was highly critical of the juvenile court system. It pointed out numerous cases in which the rights of young people had been flagrantly abused.

Though the *Monitor's* charges sound extreme, they appear to be supported by the facts. In South Carolina, for example, children often are sent to reform schools without their parents knowing it. A juvenile may be taken into custody at night, jailed, led before a judge early the next morning, and hauled off to reform school in handcuffs before noon. Reform school officials then telephone the child's parents at home and tell them he will be locked up for several months. Such procedures are not uncommon, says George Compton, superintendent of the South Carolina School for (Delinquent) Girls.

Compton recalls a typical case in which five boys from "substantial families" in the neighboring state of North Carolina were arrested in Myrtle Beach, South Carolina. They were charged with siphoning gasoline from an automobile in order to have enough fuel to drive home. It took lawyers "three or four months" to get the boys released and sent home, Compton says.

In many areas, crowded juvenile court dockets result in children being held in reform schools for prolonged periods while their cases are pending. Such juveniles have not even been declared delinquent, but they are deprived of their freedom just the same. In Providence, Rhode Island, although children are rarely committed to the reform school, the institution is constantly full. Its occupants are mainly juveniles who are being held until the courts take up their cases. Some of them are held for a year or more without ever being declared delinquent. On one recent occasion, only 5 of the school's 186 children had been legally committed as delinquents.

Many legal experts contend that such a system is unconstitutional. Rhode Island authorities defend the procedure on the ground that it is intended for the long-range benefit of the child. They explain that, if a child is committed to a reform school as a delinquent, he must carry this stigma with him for life. But if he is simply held for a time while his case is pending and then released without being declared delinquent, his reputation is theoretically protected. Such a system, no matter how noble its motives, carries obvious hazards to a juvenile's rights. It is far from unlikely that a youth, wrongly accused of delinquency, might be held for a long period before being given the chance to prove his innocence.

In some states, children are ordered taken to reform schools without ever appearing in court. The *Christian Science Monitor* series reported documented cases of this sort in the state of Washington and in Iowa. One such case occurred in Ames, Iowa, the *Monitor* said. It arose when the secretary to a probation officer went to a beer party in a nearby town. At the party, she saw a boy who had previously been placed under a suspended commitment—meaning that he could remain free as long as he behaved, but could be sent to reform school if the juvenile court judge found evidence of further misconduct. Presumably, attendance at a beer party could be regarded as misconduct. "The secretary called her employer [the probation officer], who picked up the boy and hauled him to the home of Judge Ed Kelley," the *Monitor* reported. "Judge Kelley signed the commitment papers [ordering the boy taken immediately to a reform school] in his driveway. The probation officer confirmed that this happened. Judge Kelley became angered when asked about the case and would only say that 'the kid had a full hearing.' "

Another source of complaints is the fact that, although the Gault decision supposedly guaranteed juveniles the right to counsel in cases where they face possible time in custody, many still face the courts without attorneys and without being aware they are entitled to representation. Numerous judges argue that their communities cannot afford to provide lawyers for indigent juveniles. But they ignore the fact that attorneys are obliged to serve, without fees or with only nominal fees, if appointed by the courts to represent the poor.

It seems clear that decisions such as the one in the Gault case, to achieve their maximum effectiveness, must be accompanied by several forms of supplementary action. Juvenile court judges must accept and put into practice the reforms ordered by the Supreme Court. If they fail to do so, lawyers and citizens must pressure them to respond. And, perhaps most important, young people must make themselves aware of their rights so they can demand proper treatment if brought before the courts.

Many experts believe the Gault decision, while carrying immense significance, still leaves room for additional reforms in the field of juvenile justice. The President's Commission on Law Enforcement and the Administration of Justice, for example, has made numerous reform proposals.

The commission has recommended that the jurisdiction of juvenile courts be narrowed. "The conduct-illegal-only-for-children category of the [juvenile] court's jurisdiction should be substantially circumscribed so that it ceases to include such acts as smoking, swearing, and disobedience to parents and comprehends only acts that entail a real risk of long-range harm to the child, such as experimenting with drugs, repeatedly becoming pregnant out of wedlock, and being habitually truant from school," the commission said. "Serious consideration, at the least, should be given to complete elimination of the court's power over children for noncriminal conduct."

The commission went beyond the terms of the Gault decision in recommending reforms aimed at assuring juveniles due process of law. It was particularly critical of the practice of keeping juveniles in custody for unreasonable periods.

Among the most difficult questions faced by juvenile courts is whether to maintain secrecy over their proceedings in order to protect the young people involved from public stigma. Some state laws forbid public disclosure of the identity of an arrested juvenile, unless he is accused of an extremely serious crime, and require that juvenile court proceedings be closed to the public and the press. But other states leave such matters to the discretion of individual judges.

Whether the commission's recommendations will be adopted is an open question. While they are being considered, other proposals for broadening the rights of young people taken before juvenile courts are also being advanced. Among the most important is the suggestion that juveniles be given the right to be tried by juries.

The U.S. Supreme Court has yet to rule directly on the subject. It had the opportunity to do so in November 1969, but sidestepped the issue. The court was asked at that time to order the release of Clarence J. Debacker of Fremont, Nebraska, who had been committed to a reformatory two years earlier at the age of seventeen for forging a thirty-dollar check on his father's bank account. Clarence's appeal to the Supreme Court argued that he had been unconstitutionally denied a jury trial by the juvenile court judge who heard his case. His appeal relied on a 1968 Supreme Court decision holding that adults accused of serious crimes in state courts must be given jury trials if they asked for them. The decision, however, provided that the right to a jury trial would not be applied retroactively to cases tried before the date of the Supreme Court ruling (May 20, 1968). Since Clarence's case had been heard by the juvenile court judge almost two months before the Supreme Court handed down its decision on jury trial for adults, the high court ruled that "this case is not an appropriate one" in which to decide the question of juveniles' jury-trial rights. Thus, young people intent on winning the right to jury trials must wait until a more appropriate case is decided by the Supreme Court—and hope it is decided in their favor— or else seek broad-scale legislation to change the current system. Their effort, in any case, faces strong opposition. The National Council of Juvenile Court Judges, among others, strenuously opposes the concept of jury trials for juveniles.

One of the chief problems confronted by those who seek expansion of young people's rights before the courts is that the general public often shows apathy or, worse, antagonism toward their aims. The current wave of activism among the young, including the resort to violent protest, has led many adults to conclude that young people need more, not fewer, restrictions. Occasionally, however, an incident occurs that succeeds in mobilizing public opinion on the side of the young. Such an event took place in late 1969 in Florida.

Two boys—Donald Douglas, fourteen, and Richard Copas, fifteen—were sentenced by a judge to serve three-year sentences in an adult prison on a variety of charges. Despite their youth and small stature (Donald weighed only eighty-four pounds), Judge Jack Rogers of Fort Pierce, Florida, ordered that they be sent to a prison with hardened criminals. Judge Rogers called the boys incorrigible— pointing out that their crimes had included truancy, chicken theft, trespassing, running away from home, stealing a horse bridle, and "entering without breaking into" a residence. "When you've got a bad apple, why keep it?" the judge said. "It was not their first offense, and all our remedies have been exhausted to show them the right way."

Under Florida law, once the boys had been convicted of a felony (which they were), they could be either sentenced to prison or placed on probation. Judge Rogers felt probation was out of the question, so he sent them to prison. His decision made front-page news across the country and stirred a storm of criticism. A news photograph of Donald, appearing even younger than his fourteen years as he sat among adult convicts at a prison reception center, whipped the storm to even greater intensity.

Dr. James Bax, secretary of Florida's Department of Health and Rehabilitative Services, expressed outrage at Judge Rogers's action. He voiced grave fears that the two boys would be subjected to sexual abuses by adult convicts, whom he described as "just animals waiting around for these kids." Bax said both Donald and Richard were the products of broken homes and their behavior, while deplorable, was also understandable. He said Donald's records showed that, as a boy of six, he had been out riding in a car with his parents one day when the father suddenly stopped, put him and his mother out, and drove away. "The father never came back," he said.

After news of the sentencing hit the papers and television, Bax was deluged with telephone calls and telegrams protesting Judge Rogers's action. He also received more than fifty messages from families across the country, offering to provide homes for the boys if they were released. Bax appealed to Florida Governor Claude Kirk, who had been on a trip abroad at the time of the sentencing, to take action to remove the boys from the adult prison.

When he heard the story, Kirk immediately flew in his private plane to Lake Butler, where the boys were imprisoned, and ordered them released in his custody. He then took them to a youthful offender facility in Tallahassee.

Although the case brought a sudden surge of attention to the plight of young people in trouble with the law, the furor soon faded. The public generally returned to a mood of indifference on the subject. And juveniles brought before the courts were once again left to fend for themselves, in the main, or to depend on their parents, many of whom were just as ill-informed as their children on questions involving young people's rights. The best protection a young person can have against violation of his rights by a law-enforcement officer or a judge is a basic knowledge of the laws that may affect him. Of course, having a capable attorney in his corner can be essential. But, unless the juvenile knows his rights, he may do his case irreparable harm before the attorney ever arrives on the scene.

It is particularly important that a young person know what to do when arrested, for the time immediately following an arrest is often the period when the most serious violations of constitutional rights occur. Assuming that a juvenile has been arrested somewhere other than his home, and that neither his parents nor friends know he is in custody, his first step upon arriving at the police station should be to ask permission to make a telephone call. Officers are required to allow at least one call, but often permit several. The call should go to the juvenile's parents, closest friend or, if the young person has one, to his lawyer. The essential information to convey is exactly where he is being held, when and where he will be taken before a judge for arraignment, and the precise charge on which he is being held. With this information, his parents, friends, or lawyer can set the wheels in motion to try to get him released on bail.

It is advisable for the person arrested to give police his correct name and address. If he doesn't, his chances of being bailed out are almost nonexistent. But, beyond his name and address, he should decline to provide any information until he has conferred with a lawyer. He should specifically avoid discussing the charges against him with the police until he has seen the lawyer. Experienced officers, while complying with recent court decisions by informing a prisoner of his rights, often try to persuade him to waive these rights. They should not be waived unless the defendant's lawyer approves—which he usually won't. If police persist in trying to question a prisoner before he has conferred with an attorney, he should decline to answer and insist on seeing his lawyer.

If no private lawyer is available, or the young person's family cannot afford to retain one, he should seek the aid of an organization such as the Legal Aid Society. Agencies such as Legal Aid provide lawyers, without charge, to persons unable to pay for legal counsel.

Once arrested, there are certain procedures to which the juvenile should submit. He should not, for example, resist being searched. The courts have held that policemen have the right to search even people who are not under arrest, if they believe such people appear suspicious or dangerous. If a person is inside his home and not under arrest, however, he has the right to refuse to allow a search unless the police produce a valid search warrant. When under arrest, a young person should comply with a police request to fingerprint him. In some cases, such as arrests on minor charges, no fingerprints may be requested. But, if they are, the prisoner will gain nothing by refusing to cooperate. In the end his fingerprints will be taken, and his recalcitrance may lead to problems in arranging bail.

When he is taken to court for arraignment, his lawyer will usually ask that the judge set bail. As previously pointed out, some juvenile courts do not grant bail. But, if bail is allowed, the amount is generally determined by the seriousness of the alleged crime and the defendant's background. If the bail is relatively low, the defendant or his family may want to post it in cash. If it is high, however, the usual practice is to seek the help of a professional-bondsman. For a fee (up to 5 percent of the designated bail), the bondsman will post the necessary security to obtain the prisoner's release—provided he feels the defendant is a good risk. The purpose of bail is to assure the defendant's later appearances in court. If the defendant fails to appear when ordered to do so, the bond may be forfeited.

When the juvenile's case comes up in court, his lawyer may move for dismissal of the charges if any of his constitutional rights have been violated, if the evidence is insufficient, or if there are mitigating circumstances. The defendant should not be afraid to confide in his lawyer. An attorney is able to provide the most effective defense when he has all possible information available to him. Under the canons of the legal profession, an attorney is forbidden to reveal information given him in confidence by his client.

By knowing what his rights are, insisting that they be respected, and following the advice of his lawyer, the young person who runs afoul of the law can be reasonably sure of protection from abuse by the police and the courts. The material in this chapter has been intended to provide general information, applicable across the board to most cases that arise in juvenile courts. Certain types of legal troubles affecting juveniles, however, such as those involving drugs and sex, pose special problems that merit detailed examination. These will be discussed in the next chapter.

SUMMARY

1. Frequent violations of young people's rights occur in cases involving alleged crimes. Minors should make themselves aware of the procedures to follow if arrested. Most important, they should recognize that, no matter how minor the alleged offense, they should consult with an attorney, since even minor criminal records may adversely affect their future lives.

2. The courts increasingly are recognizing that minors in custody are entitled to rights comparable to those accorded in criminal cases, such as the right to counsel, the right to confront and cross-examine witnesses, etc.

3. The juvenile court system, in most sections of the country, is in need of major reforms. Many judges handling juvenile cases do not even hold law degrees. Agencies such as the Legal Aid Society, the American Civil Liberties Union, and some bar associations are trying to remedy the situation.

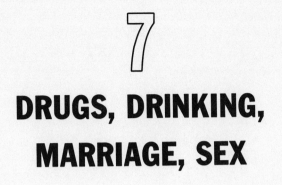

7

DRUGS, DRINKING, MARRIAGE, SEX

AS must be obvious to anyone who has considered the subject even casually, the illegal use of drugs has increased enormously in recent years. Just how enormously is illustrated with a few statistics. In 1958 there were nearly 10,000 arrests throughout the country on drug charges. By 1968, the number had soared to 162,000. And those figures, of course, did not even take into account the thousands of persons who used drugs illegally but escaped detection by law-enforcement officers.

Equally revealing were the figures showing the relative ages of those arrested. They bolstered the widely held beliefs that the greatest increase in drug use has been among young people and that young people now account for the majority of narcotics law violators. In 1958 3.8 percent of those arrested on drug charges were under eighteen years of age; 14.7 percent were under twenty-one, and 35.1 percent were under twenty-five. But, ten years later, the figures showed that 26.6 percent of those arrested were under eighteen; 56.5 percent were under twenty-one, and 76.6 percent were under twenty-five. In 1958, there were virtually no drug arrests involving children younger than fifteen. By 1968, 3 percent of those arrested were fifteen or younger.

Such terms as "drugs," "narcotics," and "dope" are often used loosely to describe a wide variety of substances, some of which may be possessed or sold legally (for example, with a doctor's prescription). The drugs that can bring arrest generally fall into such categories as hallucinogens (those that can cause hallucinations) such as LSD and to a lesser extent marijuana, depressants such as heroin, cocaine, and certain barbiturates, and stimulants such as pep pills.

Current laws restricting the use of some drugs and banning the use of others are, of course, subjects of intense controversy. Campaigns are under way in various sections of the country, for example, to legalize marijuana. This book is not an appropriate forum in which to argue the merits of the current laws and the attempts to liberalize them. It is, however, an appropriate place in which to discuss young people's rights under the existing laws.

The general laws affecting criminal conduct by young people—and protection of their rights—also govern alleged drug violations. But the peculiar nature of the drug traffic, and the ways in which law-enforcement officers try to combat it, present several special problems that are not common to most other forms of criminal activity.

In investigating suspected drug "pushers," for instance, it is common for law-enforcement agencies to make use of undercover men. These officers, dressed in plain clothes and posing as prospective narcotics purchasers, try to infiltrate groups suspected of using and/or selling drugs. Often, they masquerade as students, seeking evidence of drug violations in and around schools. Their aim generally is to make a narcotics "buy" from one of the suspects, which may then be used as the basis of a criminal prosecution.

The rules of evidence concerning such transactions are designed, in part, to protect the rights of the suspect. In order for authorities to prosecute an alleged narcotics seller on the basis of a "buy" made by an undercover man, there usually must be a witness to the sale. The undercover man's testimony that he made such a "buy" is generally considered insufficient to sustain a criminal case in the absence of supporting testimony by someone else. Therefore, agents almost always work in teams of at least two when arranging a "buy." The second agent may not actually be involved in the transaction, but he must be in sufficiently close proximity to see the drugs change hands.

The law also provides protection for the suspect against "entrapment." That is, it prohibits peace officers from deliberately luring a suspect into a violation of the law and then arresting him for it. An example of "entrapment" might work this way: An undercover man, posing as a potential buyer, might persuade a suspect to obtain narcotics from a third party, previously unknown to the suspect. In the absence of persuasion from the undercover man, the suspect would never have bought the drugs from the third party. But, in the hope of reselling the narcotics to the undercover man, the suspect might make the "buy." If the authorities tried to prosecute the suspect on the basis of such a "buy," he could make a valid claim of "entrapment" and probably have the case dismissed.

A 1969 decision by the U.S. Supreme Court provided additional safeguards for suspects in marijuana cases. For more than three decades, federal authorities had been prosecuting defendants under drug laws that made it illegal to possess or transfer marijuana without paying a $100-per-ounce tax and also made it a crime to import marijuana from abroad without proper authority. The Supreme Court's 1969 ruling declared such provisions unconstitutional.

The decision came in a case involving Dr. Timothy Leary, the controversial enthusiast of hallucinogenic drugs, and his teen-aged daughter, Susan. In 1966, Leary and his daughter had been caught entering Laredo, Texas, from Mexico with several ounces of marijuana in their automobile. They were charged with failure to pay the $100-per-ounce tax and failure to obtain government permission before importing the marijuana. Both were convicted in a federal court trial. Leary was given a five-to-thirty-year prison sentence and Susan, then eighteen, was placed on probation until the age of twenty-one. They appealed their convictions first to the U.S. Fifth Circuit Court of Appeals in New Orleans and then to the Supreme Court. The Supreme Court upheld the appeals, reversing the convictions and declaring the laws under which they had been tried invalid. (Another case against Leary, however, was sustained and he was sentenced to prison for that conviction.)

The court reasoned that the law imposing the tax on marijuana was unconstitutional because it forced anyone paying the tax, in effect, to incriminate himself under various state narcotics laws. The tax law required anyone planning to buy marijuana to prepay the $100-per-ounce tax and declare to the federal government his intention of making the purchase. Such information was then made available to state officials. Since all fifty states have laws making marijuana possession illegal, anyone complying with the federal law subjected himself to prosecution under the state laws. The Supreme Court held that the federal law thus violated the constitutional principle that nobody should be compelled to provide evidence incriminating himself.

As for the federal law making it illegal to import marijuana from abroad without government permission, the Supreme Court held invalid the theory under which authorities had prosecuted Leary and other defendants. The theory was that anyone possessing marijuana in the United States must be presumed to know that it had been imported, since at least 90 percent of all marijuana seized in this country had been found to have been grown in Mexico. Although marijuana grows in many areas of the United States, prosecutors contend it is of inferior quality and is rarely smoked by knowledgeable drug users. The Supreme Court, ruled in reversing the initial decision that it was not fair to assume the average marijuana smoker knew his marijuana had probably been imported from Mexico. It thus declared the law unconstitutional.

But the Supreme Court decision still left in force numerous federal and state laws prohibiting the use of marijuana and other drugs. In fact, there is currently such a hodgepodge of laws, providing inconsistent penalties for various drug violations, that the Nixon administration has proposed new federal legislation aimed at making the regulations more rational. The administration proposals, if enacted by Congress, would generally reduce the penalties imposed on drug users while providing stiffer sentences for professional narcotics traffickers.

For example, under present federal law, a first offender convicted of marijuana possession is subject to a prison sentence of two to ten years. A second offender faces a mandatory sentence of five to twenty years. Under the administration's proposal, a first offender would be subject to a maximum of one year and, under a special provision, would be eligible for immediate probation. If he got through the probation period without encountering further troubles with the law, the first offender would be allowed to escape without a criminal record. A second marijuana offense, under the administration proposal, would bring a maximum of two years in prison and a $10,000 fine.

Under present law, anyone distributing narcotics to others, even if he makes no profit, is subject to a mandatory sentence of five to twenty years for a first offense. The administration proposal contains a special provision applying to young people who are not professional peddlers. If caught distributing "a small amount of marijuana for no remuneration," they would be subject to a maximum sentence of one year. But anyone distributing drugs for profit would be subject to a five-year term on the first offense and ten years on subsequent offenses. Anyone distributing drugs for profit to a person under eighteen years of age would face a ten-year maximum on the first and all subsequent offenses. In addition, "professional criminals" convicted of large-scale narcotics trafficking would be subject to life imprisonment and $100,000 fines. One of the more controversial provisions of the administration plan would authorize federal agents to break into homes or offices without notice on narcotics raids if they had reason to believe those inside would destroy illicit drug supplies if notice were given.

At this writing, the administration bill has been passed by the Senate but is still pending in the House of Representatives. It apparently faces some opposition in the House. But, even if the House does not approve the precise proposals advanced by the administration, it is expected to pass a measure aimed at achieving the same general purposes—relaxing the laws against drug users while cracking down on professional traffickers. The Nixon administration hopes that the new federal legislation, which would not apply to arrests made by local and state police, may serve as a model for revision of existing state laws.

That hope, however, may prove to be nothing more than wishful thinking. The increase in drug use has prompted some state legislatures to pass new laws imposing stiffer, not lighter, penalties even for possession of small amounts of marijuana. Among the states to tighten their laws were New York, Montana, Maine, Indiana, and Utah. Montana, for example, increased the penalties for possession and sale of drugs, including marijuana. Indiana passed five laws governing criminal cases involving drugs and also adopted a far-reaching new law outside the criminal area. That law makes it unlawful for schools to employ anyone addicted to drugs and requires annual physical examinations for all school employees to assure that they do not use drugs.

The wide disparity in penalties imposed for drug use by various state court judges is a common source of complaint. In some states, for example, a professional heroin peddler may be let off with a suspended sentence or brief jail term. Yet, in a recent Texas case, a twenty-one-year-old man was sentenced under state law to fifty years in prison for the sale of two marijuana cigarettes—which federal researchers said contained the "high" potential of perhaps three martinis.

One response to complaints about unfairly severe sentences has been consideration of a plan under which first offenders in drug cases would not be arrested, but rather placed in rehabilitation programs. Such a plan is currently being drawn up by the legislative committee of the New York State Police Chiefs Association for submission to the state legislature. Similar proposals are being studied in other states. Under the plan being considered in New York, police would not arrest a first offender if he agreed to be isolated from his usual environment and to undergo re-habilitative treatment. Francis B. Looney, president of the New York State Police Chiefs Association, explained that the isolation provision was intended both to benefit the offender and to prevent him from "contaminating" others. Looney said he felt current drug laws gave police too little discretion in the drug field. "If we have evidence of a crime, we must arrest—even though we know the tragic consequences of an arrest record for young people," he said.

For every proposal such as Looney's, however, there seems to be another by someone else that would initiate more repressive regulations against young people suspected of using drugs. Shortly before Looney put forward his plan, for example, some of his neighboring public officials on Long Island (where he serves as Nassau County police commissioner) recommended that school officials be required to subject students to blood and urine tests aimed at determining whether they use drugs. The recommendation was made by the town board in Smithtown, Long Island, and a local narcotics guidance council. Although parents' consent would be required before such tests could be given, many observers questioned the legality and effectiveness of such a plan. Some pointed out that two of the drugs used most commonly by young people, marijuana and LSD, could not be detected through urine and blood tests. Even more fundamental were the arguments that the tests would violate students' rights. Aryeh M. Neier, executive director of the New York chapter of the American Civil Liberties Union, said such tests would violate the students' rights to avoid incriminating themselves. "The school would become part of the criminal investigative process," Neier said. "We will bring suit [against the appropriate school district] if a pupil is given the test." At this writing, such tests have not yet been inaugurated, but there is no clear evidence that they will be permanently avoided.

With the increasing concern over drug abuse among young people, it is hard to predict what course the future will take—more permissive or more restrictive government policies. For the moment, the most that can be said is that young people must learn to live within the existing laws or be prepared to face the consequences of activities that society (rightly or wrongly) has branded as illegal.

Issues parallel to that of drug use are those dealing with the right of minors to drink alcoholic beverages. State laws on the subject vary widely, and in some cases provisions allow drinking on a local-option basis. A table covering drinking ages and requirements will be found in the appendix.

Another area in which young people frequently find themselves at odds with the legal and moral codes espoused by adult society is the field of sexual conduct. Here, again, it is not the purpose of this book to discuss the relative merits of such codes. Suffice it to say that there is a great deal of hypocrisy among adults, as well as young people, on the subject of sex. Moreover, there is an abundance of mythology on the subject. Many young people, perhaps because of embarrassment, refrain from asking pertinent questions about their rights in the field of sexual conduct. Instead, they accept the ill-informed street gossip of their friends. Thus, myths are not only perpetuated but given ever wider currency.

Any discussion of the legal aspects of young people's sexual conduct ought to mention briefly, at the very least, that a double standard of sorts exists on such matters in the United States. The double standard involves the attitudes of many adults. While they advocate strict adherence to the laws on sexual activities by young people, such people ignore the fact that hundreds of thousands of their fellow adults frequently violate laws governing adult sexual conduct. Many states, for example, have laws making fornication and adultery by adults criminal acts punishable by imprisonment and/or fines. But such laws are rarely, if ever, enforced. And, if they were, the outcry from the public would likely be thunderous. Yet, many of the same people who blithely ignore such laws are in the vanguard of those decrying "the loose sexual morals" of today's young people.

Young people may decry the double standard, with just cause, but there appears to be little they can do to change the minds of the adults. For the time being, at least, they seemingly must learn to live with the system or be prepared to pay the penalty for defying it. The penalty is more of a threat to them than it is to adults defying sexual taboos. For, while the laws affecting young people's sexual conduct are not universally enforced, they are certainly enforced more frequently than those governing adults.

A case in point is the legal issue of statutory rape. Most states have laws making it a crime—namely, statutory rape —for a male to have sexual intercourse with a female who is under the age of consent. The age of consent varies from state to state, from twenty-one down. It makes no difference under the statutory-rape laws whether the female willingly participates in the sexual acts, rather than being forced or coerced. The laws assume she is too young to give her consent. The male may be considered just as guilty in having sexual relations with her as if he had forced her to submit by brute strength. Obviously, such laws are very difficult to enforce. If the police were to try to investigate the behavior of all young people suspected of having sexual relations, they would have time for little else. But, if a young female or her parents file a complaint, the police are obliged to investigate. Charges of statutory rape are not to be taken lightly. In some states, the law provides the same maximum penalties for statutory rape as for forcible rape. These penalties include, in a few cases, the possibility of a death sentence, though in practice such a sentence is almost never handed down.

In addition to the laws on statutory rape, laws prohibiting adults from "contributing to the delinquency of a minor" are also used to govern young people's sexual conduct. Such laws are subject to broad interpretation, covering numerous other forms of conduct besides sexual activities. Generally, any act by an adult that can reasonably be interpreted as leading a juvenile directly into illegal activities may be considered as "contributing to the delinquency of a minor." In the field of sexual conduct, such laws sometimes have been invoked to prosecute adults who have engaged in sex play, short of actual intercourse, with minors. The minors, in such circumstances, are subject to possible charges of juvenile delinquency. Although most people tend to think in terms of only male adults being charged with "contributing to the delinquency of a minor" as a result of sexual activities, female adults are just as susceptible to prosecution under the law. A female adult who indulges in sexual relations or sex play with a minor is by no means immune from prosecution. While far fewer females than males have been arrested in such cases, there have nonetheless been numerous incidents in which females have been prosecuted.

No matter what laws are imposed, of course, there will be some who will break them. This is especially so in a field such as that of sexual conduct. As many observers are fond of contending, "you can't legislate morals." (They often point to this country's ill-fated experiment with prohibition of alcoholic beverages to support their argument.) Assuming that some—indeed, many—young people are going to violate the laws on sexual conduct, the question then becomes what to do about the consequences. Specifically, what happens when an unmarried young girl becomes pregnant? What laws and other regulations apply to her? What about the father of her unborn child?

If the girl does not want to have the baby, she faces legal problems in obtaining an abortion virtually everywhere in the United States except Hawaii, New York, California, and the District of Columbia. Thirty-eight states currently enforce laws prohibiting doctors from performing abortions unless the life (or in some cases the health) of the mother would be endangered by giving birth. Nine other states—Arkansas, Colorado, Delaware, Georgia, New Mexico, North Carolina, Maryland, Kansas, and Oregon—have liberalized their laws to permit abortions to preserve the mother's mental health or when the pregnancy is the result of rape or incest or when there is a risk the child may be born deformed. But by and large—except in Hawaii, New York, California, and the District of Columbia—it is difficult to obtain a legal abortion. Even those four jurisdictions enforced anti-abortion laws until recently.

In November 1969 the District of Columbia law was struck down by Federal District Judge Gerhard A. Gessell in the case of a physician charged with illegally performing an abortion. The judge ruled that the law, which permitted abortions only when necessary "for the preservation of the mother's life or health," was unconstitutionally vague. The California Supreme Court overturned that state's law on similar grounds. Advocates of nationwide abortion-law reform hope to use the California and District of Columbia decisions to attack statutes in other sections of the country. But, at this writing, the rulings are applicable only in California and the District of Columbia.

In February 1970 the Hawaii State Legislature repealed the state's 101-year-old abortion law and passed new legislation permitting an expectant mother to get an abortion simply because she did not want to have a baby. Hawaii thus became the only state in the country to adopt such legislation. Its law contained only a few restrictions: The expectant mother must be a resident of the state for at least ninety days before the operation is performed; the abortion must be performed in a hospital by a doctor licensed by the state; and the operation must take place within the first five months of pregnancy. The law leaves the decision on whether to have an abortion clearly in the hands of the expectant mother.

Of course, thousands of illegal abortions are performed each year in every section of the country. The expectant mothers who have such operations performed take grave risks. Not only are they violating the law; in many cases they are jeopardizing their lives, since illegal abortionists often are not trained doctors or are operating under unsafe conditions.

Assuming that an unmarried expectant mother elects to go through with the birth of her child—because she actually wants the baby, cannot arrange an abortion, or for other reasons—she faces a variety of possible official restrictions on her future life. Many high schools, for example, prohibit girls from attending once their pregnancies have been discovered. Some ban such girls from returning to school after they have given birth. Since the mid-1960s, several cities across the country, recognizing that bans of this kind might violate the girls' rights to public education and almost certainly retarded their chances to lead relatively normal lives, have begun "comprehensive services" programs for unwed mothers. Most of the programs are centered around special high schools for pregnant girls. In addition to the usual high school courses, such schools generally provide the girls with counseling services and instruction on how to care for themselves and their babies during and after pregnancy.

In the New York City school system, where 2,487 pregnancies were reported among girls from the seventh through the twelfth grades during the 1968–1969 academic year, there are five special schools for expectant mothers. A pregnant girl is not compelled to attend such a school. Unlike many other cities, New York allows expectant mothers to continue going to their home schools if they choose, unless their doctors want them removed. But, for every pregnant New York student who elects to stay in her home school, there are five who choose the special schools.

"The girls seem to feel more secure when they are with other young ladies who have the same problem," says Daniel Schreiber, an assistant school superintendent who heads the program under which the five special schools are administered. The students' courses include English, social science, home economics, business education, science, math, and special instruction by a nurse on baby care and birth control.

In January 1970 the problems of teen-aged parents, both married and unmarried, were explored at a National Conference on Parenthood in Adolescence in Washington, D.C. About four hundred social workers and doctors at the conference heard a dozen young mothers and expectant mothers describe the obstacles they faced. "Some of the old folks kind of make me mad the way they turn up their noses," said an unwed expectant mother named Jan. "A nurse told me, 'You're too young to have a baby.' The way I figure, that's evidently not true because I am going to have a baby." Another unmarried girl said: "I want the baby, my mother wants it, and my boyfriend wants it. So there's nothing wrong with it."

The girls gave varying accounts of why they had become pregnant. "It was revenge," one of them said. "I never had done anything before; I'd been an angel." Another said: "Suppose your boyfriend is going into the service. He might get killed in Vietnam, and you might want something to remember him by."

The unmarried girls spoke with some bitterness about their difficulties in finding jobs; two of them said they had been fired when their employers had discovered they were pregnant. Others told of their troubles in trying to return to normal lives. "We should get back in society and I think we can," one of them said. "But something's got to give, and we're not in a position to do the giving."

Marion Howard of the Yale University School of Medicine, who organized the conference, said government and private agencies must provide young parents with help in such fields as health, education, and social adjustment.

"The field used to be unwed mothers and the problem used to be illegitimacy," Miss Howard said. "Now, people are recognizing that the problem is childbearing at a very young age, and it doesn't matter whether the girl is married."

Dr. Charles Gershenson, who obtained a federal grant to open an experimental school for pregnant students, said programs such as the one he headed were making significant progress but still had a long way to go. "We're not doing nearly enough yet with the (unwed) father, and not always following through with the mother after she has her baby," he said.

A similar conference in New York pointed up another problem faced by unwed mothers: attempts by government and private agencies to make them give up their children for adoption. If an unwed mother can be shown to be unable or unwilling to care for her child, most states have legal machinery to allow the baby to be taken from her. In some cases, even when the mother seems able and willing to provide the necessary care, efforts are made to take the baby away.

Such efforts were assailed at the New York conference by Mrs. Patricia Garland Morisey, associate professor of the Fordham University School of Social Service. She challenged the assertion that children born out of wedlock were necessarily unwanted. She said that many unwed mothers wanted their babies and that many unwed fathers were very concerned about what happened to their children. "If you're child-centered, you believe in people," Mrs. Morisey said. "How can you tell a girl that she should give up something that's part of the family just because you don't like the way it started?"

Even when young people want to get married (regardless

of whether a pregnancy is involved), their ages often place obstacles in their paths. All states have laws setting age requirements for marriage, with or without parents' permission.

Forty-four states require males to be twenty-one to marry without parental consent. Two, Hawaii and New Hampshire, allow them to marry without such consent at the age of twenty. Georgia permits them to marry at nineteen, and Michigan, North Carolina, and South Carolina at eighteen. Females are permitted to marry without parental consent at the age of eighteen in thirty-five states. Georgia requires them to be nineteen and Hawaii requires them to be twenty. They must wait until twenty-one to marry without parental permission in Connecticut, Florida, Kentucky, Louisiana, Mississippi, Nebraska, Ohio, Pennsylvania, Rhode Island, Tennessee, Virginia, West Virginia, and Wyoming.

Thirty-four states require males to be eighteen to marry, even with their parents' consent. New Hampshire permits them to marry with consent at fourteen, Missouri at fifteen, and Alabama, Mississippi, and Washington state at seventeen. Colorado, Connecticut, Maine, New York, North Carolina, Pennsylvania, South Carolina, Tennessee, Texas, and Utah require them to be sixteen. Michigan has no legal provision covering a male's marriage with parental permission.

Thirty-eight states allow females to marry, with parents' permission, at sixteen. New Hampshire permits them to do so at thirteen; Alabama, South Carolina, Texas, and Utah at fourteen; and Mississippi, Missouri, North Dakota, Oklahoma, and Oregon at fifteen. The state of Washington requires them to be seventeen and Kansas requires them to be eighteen.

Perhaps the most uncharted legal area concerning young people and sex is the field involving their exposure to spicy literature, motion pictures, plays, and the like. Although numerous court cases have been decided in the field of obscenity, most of them have involved the rights of adults to read or view purportedly salacious material. Even those growing out of arrests of adults on charges of selling obscene literature to minors or admitting minors to purportedly obscene motion pictures have been directly concerned with the legal rights of the adults, not the rights of the juveniles. No significant cases have yet been decided on the question of a minor's rights to read or view such material, if he chooses.

Most states have laws forbidding the sale of obscene literature to young people and prohibiting their admission to purportedly lewd motion pictures and stage performances. The laws are enforced generally against the purveyors, such as the booksellers and the theater operators. But their effect is to deny the young person the right to read or see material available to adults.

In addition to laws, teen-agers are confronted with such restrictions as those imposed by the movie industry's self-devised code on "audience suitability." The code, sponsored by the Motion Picture Association of America and other industry groups, rates motion pictures under one of four categories. The "G" category applies to films the industry decides should be available to moviegoers of all ages. The "GP" category permits viewers of all ages to be admitted to the theaters, but suggests that parental guidance be used. The "R" category applies to films barred to persons under seventeen years of age "unless accompanied by parent or adult guardian." The "X" rating applies to films flatly banned for everyone under seventeen or eighteen, depending on the geographic area in which the particular theater is situated.

Some qualified observers feel that young people could successfully challenge the movie rating system and laws restricting their access to materials dealing with sex if they decided to go to court. They suggest, for example, that civil rights legislation barring discrimination in places of public accommodation such as theaters could be applied to age discrimination as well as racial discrimination. One fifteen-year-old boy in New York State recently studied the state laws and discovered none of them set age requirements on most films distributed within the state. Since he was barred by the movie industry code from attending many movies, he consulted a local district attorney on his legal rights. The district attorney advised him he would have a "fighting chance" to upset the rating system if he went to court. Thus far, he has not done so; nor has anyone else.

But, in this era of expanding rights for young people, the day is probably not far off when this and other undecided questions regarding minors' rights in the area of sexual conduct will be taken to the courts. Judging by recent history, such legal tests seem certain to further broaden the spectrum of legal rights available to young people.

SUMMARY

1. More than half the Americans arrested on drug charges are under twenty-one, and the number of young people involved in drug cases increases virtually every year.

2. The current trend in law-enforcement is to reduce penalties for drug users while increasing them for sellers.

3. Laws governing sexual conduct are more tightly enforced in the cases of juveniles than of adults. Such laws involve those concerning, for example, statutory rape and "contributing to the delinquency of a minor." While the fairness of such enforcement may be subject to challenge, young people must learn their rights under the laws or face possibly serious consequences.

4. All states have laws setting minimum ages for marriage, with or without parental consent. The minimum age in the United States for marriage with parents' permission is thirteen (for girls) and fourteen (for boys), as provided by state law in New Hampshire. Other state laws vary widely.

HOME AND PARENTS

$\mathbb{O}$F all the legal questions arising over the rights of young people, probably the most difficult to solve concern the relationships between minors and their parents. The special nature of the family as an institution, the emotional factors involved, the psychological implications, and numerous other elements all combine to make the dinner table a much more appropriate forum than the legislature or the court for the solution of such questions. But there are occasions when the young person must look to the law for protection of his rights in dealing with his parents.

Although numerous laws are designed to protect young people, relatively few are written in such a way as to preclude parents' prerogatives to rear their children as they see fit. These few fall chiefly in the area protecting young people from serious physical abuse or neglect by their parents. State laws do not, for example, attempt to interfere with a parent's right to impose reasonable punishment, such as spanking, on a child. But they do prohibit a parent from beating a child so severely that he needs medical attention.

Many of the legal rights of minors, in relation to their parents, are not derived from laws drawn up by legislative bodies. They flow, instead, from what is known as "decisional law"—law produced by judges' rulings in various court cases. Most states recognize, for instance, the right of a child to be supported, protected, and maintained by his parents at least until the age of eighteen. But there are relatively few laws passed by state legislatures outlining such rights; they are derived chiefly from custom and "decisional law."

Similarly, there are few laws on the statute books denying children the right to run away from home. But numerous court decisions have upheld parents' authority to have the police bring home their runaway minor children if they can be found. One prominent federal judge was asked recently whether he thought an adolescent had the right to run away from home. He replied: "An adolescent has the right to run away as far and as fast as his feet will carry him—until his parents catch up with him."

Sometimes, it takes a particularly revolting example of violation of a child's rights to bring remedial action by the government. Such was the case in New York recently on the issue of physical abuse of children by their parents. The plight of abused children—for decades a subject that was ignored by the general public and discussed only gingerly by such professionals as doctors and social workers —began to receive national attention several years ago. Campaigns to protect children from parental abuse were launched in various parts of the country, including New York. Some advances were made in New York, but the inadequacy of the state's program was soon made apparent.

The vehicle for this exposure was the tragic case of a three-year-old girl named Roxanne Felumero. On March 25, 1969, Roxanne's body was found in the East River off Manhattan. She had been beaten to death and her pockets had been filled with rocks. The mystery of who had killed Roxanne was soon solved. Her stepfather, George Poplis, a forty-one-year-old drug addict, was convicted of her murder and sentenced to twenty years to life in prison. But the solution of the murder itself told only part of the story. Perhaps more significant, from the long-range view, was the question of why Roxanne had been in the custody of her mother and stepfather at the time of her death.

The child's mother, Mrs. Marie Poplis, was also a drug addict. When Roxanne was ten months of age, her custody was relinquished by her mother and she was placed in the care of the New York Foundling Hospital. The hospital later placed her in the custody of foster parents, Mr. and Mrs. Michael Boccio of Deer Park, Long Island. Roxanne was under the supervision of New York's Family Court from the time she left the custody of her mother. She remained with Mr. and Mrs. Boccio until four months before her death. Then, in December 1968, the Family Court ordered her returned to the custody of her mother and stepfather.

During the Christmas season of 1968 Mr. and Mrs. Boccio visited Roxanne at the home of her mother and stepfather. The Boccios noticed bruises on the child's body. They reported the bruises to the Foundling Hospital, which in turn brought them to the attention of the Family Court. A medical examination disclosed that Roxanne had sixteen bruises on her buttocks, a bruise over her left eye, and a bruise on the side of her head. Since the indications were that someone (presumably her mother or stepfather) was mistreating Roxanne, a family court hearing was conducted to determine whether she should remain in their custody.

At the hearing, a representative of the Foundling Hospital made no recommendation to Judge Sylvia J. Liese on whether Roxanne should be taken away from her mother and stepfather. Despite the fact that a medical report on Roxanne's bruises was in the possession of the hospital—and despite the fact that the hospital had brought the apparent mistreatment to the attention of the court—the hospital representative later claimed: "I didn't take the position that this was an abused child." Moreover, the hospital and various other public and private agencies were supposed to have conducted investigations of the backgrounds of Mr. and Mrs. Poplis in order to help the court decide what should be done with Roxanne. Such investigations, if they were actually made, later appeared to be woefully inadequate. They failed to disclose to the court, among other things, that both the mother and stepfather were drug addicts. (Earlier, in recommending originally that Roxanne be returned from the Boccios to her mother and stepfather, the hospital had supposedly investigated Mr. and Mrs. Poplis and reported that "no court supervision was necessary" at the Poplis home.)

At the conclusion of the hearing, Judge Liese ruled that Roxanne should remain in the custody of her mother and stepfather. Two months later Roxanne was dead.

Her murder, and the apparent mishandling of her custody case, created a furor. Angry accusations were hurled by various participants in the case, including representatives of the Foundling Hospital and the Family Court, each blaming the other. Dr. Vincent J. Fontana, medical director of the hospital, claimed the Family Court should not have left Roxanne in the custody of Mr. and Mrs. Poplis because "a mountain of evidence" indicated they were not fit to care for the child. Family Court Judge Justine W. Polier, who had handled early proceedings in the case before turning jurisdiction over to Judge Liese, replied by accusing the hospital of neglecting its duty.

Because of the turmoil created by the case, and the apparent need for revision in the system used to protect children from parental abuse in New York State, the Appellate Division of the State Supreme Court ordered an intensive investigation. The investigation was conducted by a committee of judges and prominent attorneys.

The committee made specific recommendations for improvements in programs aimed at avoiding parental abuse and providing the Family Court with more effective means of deciding custody cases.

At the same time the judicial committee was conducting its investigation, other agencies were examining the general subject of child abuse as a result of Roxanne's death. They found that nearly one thousand child-abuse cases had been reported to the New York State Department of Social Services during the previous year, and they estimated that many thousands more had gone unreported. In thirty-six of the reported cases, the abused children had died. One four-year-old had died of starvation and neglect. An eighteen-month-old child had been hanged by her wrists and savagely whipped with a belt, then cut down and left to lie on the bathroom floor with a broken arm for almost two days. Others had been left permanently crippled, blind, and retarded as a result of vicious beatings by parents, stepparents, and guardians.

In the aftermath of the various investigations, both the New York State Legislature and the Appellate Division of the State Supreme Court acted to provide children greater protection from parental abuse. The legislature passed a bill creating a special branch of the Family Court to deal only with child-abuse cases. The bill also set up new machinery for swift collection of information concerning suspected incidents of abuse. The Appellate Division of the State Supreme Court, for its part, ordered a complete reorganization of the Family Court. It adopted many of the recommendations of the committee appointed to investigate Roxanne's death—providing for more effective investigations, continuous consideration of a case by one judge (rather than fragmentary supervision by several), and additional manpower assigned to child-abuse cases.

Thus, although it took a tragedy to prompt the action, New York moved to provide long-overdue guarantees of protection of young people's rights. Many states have not yet made progress in the field of child abuse that even approaches New York's. Some have done far more to prevent cruelty to animals than cruelty to children. Young people and their adult supporters must wage concentrated campaigns in such areas if they expect to bring about reforms comparable to those made in New York.

Laws merely making it illegal for parents to abuse their children have often been found insufficient. In addition to the laws, there must be effective enforcement machinery. Special legislation sometimes is necessary to make the system work. In some areas, doctors have been reluctant to report suspected cases of child abuse to government officials for fear they may be sued by the parents involved. To overcome this problem, several states have passed laws giving physicians immunity from suits in such cases. Officials emphasize that it is every citizen's duty, if he sees evidence of abuse of a child, to report it to the proper authorities. They say the citizen should not take the attitude that he may be considered a busybody or that such matters are none of his business. A child's life may well be at stake. In addition, a minor who is old enough to speak for himself should not hesitate to report his parents if they physically abuse him. This does not mean minors should call local police or welfare agency officials about petty grievances against their parents, authorities point out. But, if a minor's health or safety is endangered by his parents, he should feel free to report them to the authorities.

Not only overt acts of abuse such as beatings should be reported but also examples of neglect. Acts of neglect are considered violations of minors' rights, just as are acts of brutality. If a parent fails to feed a child properly for prolonged periods or leaves a small child alone in the home, helpless to protect himself against fire and other hazards, the parent may be taken to court on criminal charges. Moreover, the court may take the child from his custody if he is found to be an "unfit" parent.

All states have courts assigned specific jurisdiction over the problems of minors. Some handle only cases involving juveniles; others have additional responsibilities as well. They are known by various names—family courts, juvenile courts, domestic relations courts, and the like. With minor variations, they function in basically the same way. Their chief function is to protect the young person and try to see that he is reared in the best possible environment. If that means taking the child away from his parents, the court may place the minor in the custody of foster parents, a public or private social agency, or an institution such as a children's shelter. In cases of divorce or legal separation between parents, the court also has responsibility for determining custody of children. In many cases, the parents themselves reach agreement on custody matters, but such settlements must be approved by the court.

All things being equal, judges usually award custody of

minor children in divorce cases to the mothers. The theory is that a mother is better able to provide care for her children than a father, partly because she is presumably trained in homemaking skills and partly because the father normally has much of his time taken up by business activities. There are numerous exceptions, of course, in which fathers are given custody. Most result from decisions by the courts that the mothers are physically, morally, or mentally unfit to care for their children. A judge may ask a child in a divorce case which parent he would prefer to have custody, but the child's answer is by no means binding.

Similarly, in a case in which a judge is considering removing a minor from the custody of his parents and placing him in a foster home or juvenile shelter, the judge is free to ignore the child's desires. Minors are generally regarded by law as incapable of making decisions of this sort regarding their own welfare. Though their opinions may be sought, final authority rests with the courts.

Until recently, in many jurisdictions foster children often were not even entitled to court hearings to determine what was best for their own welfare. For example, if a social agency were given custody of a child by the parents, it was common practice for the agency to place the child wherever it wished—with foster parents or in an institution. If the agency later decided to move the child elsewhere, it was considered free to do so without consulting anyone else. No court hearing was required. A 1970 court decision in New York State, however, promises to change this system, not only in New York but perhaps in other states as well.

The decision came in a case involving a ten-year-old boy, Robert Tomaskow, and his eight-year-old sister, Karin. In

1964, the children's parents had been sent to jail for permitting a third child, a three-year-old girl, to starve to death. When their parents were imprisoned, Robert and Karin were shuffled among a series of foster homes by the Westchester County Social Services Department. Then, in 1966, the department placed them in the home of foster parents, Don and Ann Ballou of Harrison, New York.

The children remained with the Ballous for the next three years. But, in December 1969, the Social Services Department decided to remove them from the Ballou home and place them in a residential school. By that time, the children's parents had been released from jail. The Social Services Department contended that Robert and Karin had "conflicting feelings" about their two sets of parents—the natural parents and the Ballous. To help them resolve the conflicts, department officials said, they felt the children needed a "neutral environment" such as the residential school. Under the system then in effect, the Social Services Department was considered authorized to order the children taken from the Ballou home and placed in the school without consulting the children, the Ballous, the courts, or anyone else.

The Ballous, however, decided to challenge the system. They filed suit in the Westchester County Family Court, contending the children were entitled to a court hearing to determine what was best for their own welfare. Family Court Judge William A. Walsh, Jr., denied the Ballous' request. He ruled that as foster parents, rather than adoptive parents, they were merely "agents" of the Social Services Department. As such, he held, they had no legal standing that permitted them to object to decisions by the department. (The Ballous, fearing that the children might be returned to their natural parents, had tried repeatedly to adopt them. Their efforts had been unsuccessful.)

Refusing to give up, the Ballous appealed Judge Walsh's decision to the Appellate Division of the State Supreme Court. The Appellate Division, in a decision hailed as a landmark by advocates of young people's rights, upheld the Ballous' contention. It held that neither the Social Services Department nor any other agency could arbitrarily decide custody questions without giving the children involved the right to a court hearing. "The custody of a child may not be controlled by the established practice of any organization, no matter how noble its motives may be," the decision said.

The appeals court decision required the commissioner of the Social Services Department to prove to the satisfaction of the Family Court that a change of custody was in a child's best interests. "No longer can the commissioner do what he pleases," said Mrs. Elaine Sheps, an attorney who represented the Ballous. Legal experts said they expected the decision in the New York case to be used as a precedent for broadening the rights of children involved in custody cases elsewhere around the country.

In recent years, one of the barometers of increased dissension between young people and their parents has been the sharp rise in the number of juveniles who run away from home. Authorities estimate that at least 500,000 American teen-agers ran away from home in 1969—a figure perhaps double the number who ran away in 1965. The so-called generation gap is blamed by many experts for the majority of runaway cases. Young people who run away from home tend to be among those who cannot communicate with their parents. As FBI Director J. Edgar Hoover puts it: "They may talk about the purchase of a new car or where to go on vacation, but when it comes to some of the really serious problems that concern the young person —like the draft, the war in Vietnam, sex, drugs—there is very little, if any, serious discussion."

When a minor runs away from home, his parents usually report the disappearance to the police. The police then issue a missing-person bulletin similar to the "wanted" posters circulated on criminal fugitives. The bulletin generally contains a photograph of the runaway, a physical description, and any other information that may help identify her. Here is a typical description taken from a missing-person bulletin issued on a runaway girl:

> White female, date of birth 4-14-54, five-foot-three, 117 pounds, long blond hair, blue eyes, wears glasses, front tooth discolored, has mole on throat. When last seen, wearing: white blouse, black Bermuda shorts, orange sneakers. This girl is a naturalist and likes to walk in the woods. She is fond of animals. She has no close friends and is not interested in rock and roll music. This girl has been missing from her home since July 11, 1969.

Such bulletins ask anyone who has information about the runaway to telephone collect to the police department in the juvenile's home town. While a missing-person bulletin doesn't carry the same legal weight as a "wanted" poster on a fugitive, it often results, directly or indirectly, in a runaway being taken into custody and held until his parents can arrange to try to have him brought home. Here is the way the process might work in a hypothetical, but typical, case.

Suppose a sixteen-year-old girl we'll call Mary Taylor runs away from her home in Kansas and hitchhikes to San Francisco (which, along with Greenwich Village, New York, serves as a mecca for runaway teen-agers). Mary's parents report her disappearance to the local police in Kansas, who circulate a missing-person bulletin. A policeman in San Francisco, who has seen a copy of the bulletin, spots Mary on the street. He may not have any legal authority to arrest her on the basis of the missing-person report, but he can usually find some other seemingly valid justification for taking her into custody. Perhaps she meets the legal definition of a vagrant, in that she has no permanent residence and/or no visible means of supporting herself. Perhaps she is living in squalid, unsafe conditions that make it seem advisable to place her under the temporary supervision of juvenile authorities. Perhaps she is violating some law or other, such as those involving drugs. If all else fails, the officer may resort to an old police standby and simply hold her for questioning.

In the meantime, police in Mary's hometown are notified that she has been found. They get in touch with her parents, who decide to fly immediately to San Francisco. Police in San Francisco arrange to hold Mary in custody until her parents arrive. At the police station, there is an emotional reunion. Mary, who still doesn't want to return home, fears she'll remain behind bars unless she leaves with her parents. Reluctantly, she goes with them.

If a lawyer had been at Mary's disposal—and if she had chosen to fight her return to Kansas in the courts—the attorney probably would have been able to find one or more violations of her rights in the police handling of the case. In all likelihood, the police did not have truly sufficient grounds to take her into custody in the first place. Even if they did, the chances are they didn't have valid reasons for holding her as long as they did. Had the attorney entered the case immediately after her arrest, he might have succeeded in getting her freed on a writ of habeas corpus before her parents' arrival from Kansas.

But, in most cases of this kind, the runaways do not have the benefit of legal counsel. And, even if they do, the odds are stacked against them. Although an attorney might prove the runaway's rights had been violated, and might even win a writ of habeas corpus providing temporary freedom from custody, his chances of permanently preventing the juvenile's return home would still be slim. Most judges take the position that runaway minors, particularly those under eighteen, are not yet ready to fend for themselves. Once their parents catch up with such young people, judges usually compel the minors to go home—sometimes under the threat that they will be confined as juvenile delinquents if they run away again.

Of course, the parents' troubles do not end with the return of their runaway children. Unless the problems that lead a child to run away in the first place can be solved or at least eased, the troubles may become even more pronounced. Perhaps Mary Taylor, for example, ran away because her parents didn't approve of the boy she was dating. Now that she's back home, do her parents have the right to bar her from continuing to see the boy? Not by specific law. But, as parents of a sixteen-year-old girl, they do have the right to exercise reasonable supervision over their daughter. And certainly no court would grant Mary an injunction barring her parents from interfering with her romance. Suppose Mary and her boyfriend decided

[137]

they wanted to get married. Without her parents' consent, they couldn't do so in Kansas until Mary reached eighteen. (The usual minimum age for females who want to get married in Kansas, with or without parental consent, is eighteen. The state law provides some exceptions to this rule, but only in cases where parental permission is granted.)

To take another hypothetical case, suppose Mary's problem was not romance but school. She couldn't stand school and wanted to drop out. Her parents, however, forbade her to do so, leading her to run away. Now that she's home, can they force her to return to classes? Probably not. Since she is sixteen, she has passed the age where she can be required to attend school. (Most states, including Kansas, require attendance until the student reaches sixteen or is graduated from high school. Five states permit students to drop out at seventeen and four at eighteen.)

As if the legal relationships between parents and children were not sufficiently perplexing, new complications were added recently through a series of court decisions. These rulings tended to hold parents responsible for certain wrongful acts committed by their children.

A typical case arose in late 1969 in New Brunswick, New Jersey. A group of youths broke into two schools during a weekend, flooded a hallway with a fire hose, broke more than one hundred windows, overturned fire extinguishers, smashed typewriters, ripped pay telephones from walls, and disconnected the electrical plugs on food freezers and ice cream machines, causing the contents to spoil. All told, damage was estimated at more than four thousand dollars. Several youths were arrested on charges of juvenile delinquency. But school board officials felt such charges were not sufficient, particularly since the school system did not have insurance coverage against vandalism. The school board demanded that the parents of the students involved in the vandalism pay for repairing the damage. Some observers doubted that the board's interpretation of the law would stand up against a legal test. But the courts upheld the board, ordering the parents to pay.

In a somewhat similar case, a jury in Mineola, Long Island, held the parents of a sixteen-year-old boy responsible for an incident in which the boy shot another youth in the head. Damages of $280,000 were assessed against Mr. and Mrs. Lowell Collins of Munsey Park, Long Island, and their son, Michael. They were ordered to pay the money to the wounded boy, fourteen-year-old Thomas Libby, and his father. Evidence in the case disclosed that Michael had been given a .22-caliber rifle by his parents at the age of nine. The parents permitted him to fire the rifle without supervision. On November 20, 1963, when Michael was ten, he fired a shot from his home. The bullet flew across the street and struck Thomas in the head, causing brain damage. Six years later, in deciding the case, the jury held that Michael's parents had been negligent and should be held responsible for their son's act.

Not only civil damages but criminal charges as well may face parents as a result of their children's wrongdoing. In one recent case, for example, a housewife was charged with homicide after her six-year-old son, playing with a pistol he had found in a closet of his home, shot a five-year-old playmate to death. The local district attorney concluded that the mother had been the responsible person in the shooting, even though she had played no direct role. Children under seven years of age are exempted by most state laws from criminal responsibility on the ground that they have not yet reached the age of reason. Since the mother had been present at the time of the shooting, and had taken no action to prevent her son from playing with the pistol, the district attorney charged her with the crime.

As should be apparent, various laws dealing with relationships between parents and their children are undergoing a period of profound change. It is logical to assume that such change will continue in the years ahead. With reason and good faith prevailing on all sides, it is to be hoped that a fair balance can be struck between the need for proper parental authority and the natural desire of young people to assert their legal rights.

SUMMARY

1. Parents generally have the right to rear their children as they see fit, provided they do not resort to serious physical abuse or neglect. Children do have legal protection against cruel, sadistic parents who, for instance, beat them so badly they require medical treatment. This does not mean, however, that a parent may not use reasonable force, such as a spanking, to discipline his child.

2. Children neglected or abused by their parents may be placed by the courts or government officials in foster homes or residential schools. Although the children may be consulted about where they would like to live, their wishes do not necessarily determine the outcome.

3. Minors, particularly those under eighteen, may be

regarded as juvenile delinquents and placed in institutions if they run away from home. In most cases, provided their parents are able to determine their whereabouts, they can be compelled to return home.

4. Parents may be held liable for damages committed by their children—for example, in cases of vandalism or automobile accidents.

THE DRAFT AND
MILITARY SERVICE

ONE of the leading causes of discontent among young Americans today obviously is the national system for recruiting, maintaining, and operating its military forces. Almost daily, the newspapers and television news programs carry fresh evidence of this discontent—burning of draft cards, sacking of draft board offices, disturbances inside military stockades, organized protests by soldiers against the authority of their superiors, publication of underground newspapers for GIs, and sensational military trials and the like.

Rebellion against a system of military authority certainly is not a recent phenomenon; it is probably as old as armies themselves. Equally as old is the tendency of military leaders to try to command blind obedience. As Frederick the Great put it more than seven hundred years ago: "If my soldiers were to begin to think, not one would remain in the ranks." Today, ever-increasing numbers of soldiers and prospective soldiers are thinking and acting independently. What perhaps makes their rebellion different from those of the past is the sheer weight of their numbers and the intensity of their resistance to authority.

Not surprisingly, the machinery of government, civilian and military, has been forced to move to remedy some of the complaints. The draft system, for example, has recently undergone a reorganization. Military authorities have given increased recognition to the constitutional rights of recruits. The courts have acted to broaden the legal guarantees afforded both military men and those subject to the draft. Yet, many critics argue that the changes made thus far have merely scratched the surface of necessary reforms. They vow to continue waging vigorous battle against the system.

Many young people, though aware of the current ferment and vaguely familiar with the major points at issue, are nonetheless remarkably ignorant of the specific laws and regulations governing the draft and military service. Their ignorance is particularly surprising in view of the fact that these laws and regulations may well determine the course of their lives—indeed, may well determine the length of their lives. It would not be stretching a point to speculate that many a young man killed in the Vietnam war, for example, might never have been drafted if he had known and exercised the full scope of his legal rights.

Thus, any discussion of the legal rights of young people must necessarily deal with their rights in relation to military service. And, to understand such rights, young people must necessarily understand the system.

First, what is the draft? In simplest terms, it is a means of compelling civilians to serve in their country's armed forces, and it is usually employed only when the nation's safety is endangered by outside enemies. The draft is by no means an American creation; it was adopted in this country long after it had been employed by many other nations. Napoleon, for instance, gained control of Europe by using a draft system to raise the largest army the world had seen up to that time. Other European countries also resorted to the draft before the United States did. In Africa, Emperor Haile Selassie of Ethiopia resorted to a virtually all-inclusive draft to defend his country against Italian invaders in 1935.

The first attempt to put a draft into effect in America was made by George Washington during the Revolution but was rejected by the Continental Congress. During the Civil War, draft laws of sorts were employed by both the Union and the Confederacy. They contained many loopholes, including provision for wealthy men to evade service by hiring substitutes to serve in their places or by paying fees to the government. The Civil War laws were so unpopular that they led to numerous riots far more destructive than most antidraft protests today. The most serious occurred in New York City from July 13–16, 1863, causing an estimated thousand casualties and $1.5 million in property damage.

Our current draft system stems basically from United States participation in World War I. The country had only about 100,000 men in military service when it declared war on Germany in 1917. A draft law increased this number to 4.3 million by the end of the war in 1918. With the armistice, the draft was shelved. But in 1940, when it appeared evident that the United States would eventually be drawn into World War II, the draft was resumed with passage by Congress of the Selective Service Act. That law, with periodic revisions made over the years, is still in effect today.

It requires every American male to register with his local draft board when he reaches the age of eighteen. Failure to register is punishable by a maximum prison sentence of five years and a $10,000 fine. Until recently, the government was considered free to prosecute someone who failed to register whenever his delinquency was discovered. But on March 2, 1970, the U.S. Supreme Court ruled that all such prosecutions must take place within five years of the defendant's eighteenth birthday. Thus, if a young man fails to register at eighteen and remains undiscovered until his twenty-third birthday, he becomes immune from prosecution.

When a young man does register for the draft, he is given a draft card. Under the law, he is required to carry the card with him at all times or face possible imprisonment. Responsibility for deciding which men are actually called into military service rests with the Selective Service System, which has national headquarters in Washington and subordinate headquarters in each state. Actual day-to-day responsibility for making the selections is the work of the four thousand local draft boards across the country. Such boards are composed of local men and women who, in theory at least, are familiar with the personal and family situations of the men whose cases they consider.

Although registration is required at eighteen, as a practical matter men are not subject to being drafted until they reach nineteen. They remain eligible for induction, at least in theory, through the age of twenty-six. Until recently, the policy was to call men for induction on an "oldest-first" basis, that is, those closest to twenty-six were drafted first. If more men were needed to fill the quotas, the draft boards would work their way progressively downward in age.

But that system was abandoned on November 26, 1969, when President Nixon signed into law a measure putting a draft-lottery system into effect. Under the lottery system, men are generally called up on a "youngest-first" basis. Those most likely to be drafted now are nineteen-year-olds. One purpose of adopting the lottery system was to eliminate the long periods of uncertainty that often faced young men waiting to learn if they would be drafted. These periods could last from the ages of nineteen through twenty-six. Under the lottery system, a potential draftee is expected to learn during his nineteenth year whether he will actually have to serve. This does not necessarily mean, however, that he will be drafted at the age of nineteen. If he is entitled to a temporary deferment—for example, a student deferment—he may not begin his military service until the deferment expires.

While the lottery system is too complex to bear detailed discussion here, a brief discussion of the process does seem appropriate. The first lottery conducted under the new law took place on December 1, 1969, at Selective Service System headquarters in Washington. A large glass bowl was filled with 366 capsules, each containing a slip of paper on which was printed a month and day of the year (366, rather than 365, to make provision for leap years). One by one, the capsules were drawn from the bowl at random and opened. The pieces of paper bearing the dates were pasted on a board in the order in which they were drawn. Potential draftees whose birthdays corresponded to the dates drawn from the bowl first stood the greatest chance of being inducted.

To illustrate: The first date chosen was September 14, the second was April 24, then December 30, then February 14. Under the lottery system, local draft boards were required to consider first for induction the eligible men in their areas who had been born on September 14. Only after disposing of the cases of all such men, either by drafting them or giving them deferments, could the boards move on to men born on April 24, then those born on December 30, then those born on February 14, and so on.

Generally, it was expected that those men whose birthdays were among the first one-third drawn would be almost certain to be drafted—unless eligible for deferment. Those whose birthdays were among the last one-third drawn were considered almost equally certain not to be inducted. Those in the middle one-third might or might not be called, depending on the particular manpower quotas of their local draft boards.

Under the 1969 law, a new lottery is to be conducted each year. But, once a young man has passed through his one year of maximum vulnerability to the draft (that is, usually his nineteenth year), he can reasonably expect to be free from selection in future years, barring an unforeseen crisis such as all-out international war.

One of the chief factors in determining whether a young man will actually be called for induction is his Selective Service classification. Depending on his eligibility for one sort of deferment or another, his draft board assigns him a classification. Such classifications, and other decisions by draft boards, are subject to appeal. Perhaps surprisingly, many young men eligible for the draft are unaware of the full range of classifications and deferments that may be available to them. Here is a summary of the classifications:

Class 1A: Available for military service.

Class 1AO: Conscientious objector available only for noncombatant military service.

Class 1C: Member of the armed forces or of the U.S. Public Health Service or U.S. Environmental Science Services Administration.

Class 1D: Qualified member of military reserve unit or student taking military training, including ROTC.

Class 1O: Conscientious objector available for civilian work contributing to the maintenance of the national health, safety, or interest.

Class 1W: Conscientious objector actually assigned to work contributing to the maintenance of the national health, safety, or interest; also includes men who have completed such work.

Class 1S: Student deferred by law until graduation from high school or attainment of the age of twenty or until the end of his academic year at college.

Class 1Y: Exempt from military service for physical, mental, or moral reasons except in periods of war or national emergency as declared by Congress.

Class 2A: Occupational deferment, applying to such occupations as that of doctor, teacher, scientist, tool and die maker, and apprentice to plumber, bricklayer, mechanic, etc.

Class 2C: Agricultural deferment.

Class 2S: Student deferment, applicable to students enrolled in college and making satisfactory progress toward a degree.

Class 3A: Deferment granted to fathers and those whose induction would cause undue hardship on dependents.

Class 4A: Deferment granted to those with sufficient prior military service and the sole surviving sons of parents who have had one or more sons die in military service.

Class 4B: Government official deferred by law.

Class 4C: Alien not currently liable for military service.

Class 4D: Minister of religion or divinity student.

Class 4F: Deferred for physical, mental, or moral reasons.

5A: Past the age of liability for military service.

Classifications are determined by draft boards on the basis of questionnaires and applications for deferments filed by the potential draftees. If a young man feels he has been improperly or unfairly treated, he may ask for a personal hearing before the draft board. Policies of various boards differ on whether he may bring witnesses or an attorney with him to such a hearing. A government appeal agent is assigned to each local board, however, and is expected to advise any potential draftee who wants help. If the young man does not get what he considers satisfaction from the local board, he may carry his case to a state appeal board and ultimately to a presidential appeal board. He may also file suit in the federal courts, challenging the decisions of draft officials.

The number of court cases arising from disputes over draft status has risen sharply in recent years. Resistance to the Vietnam war, general disenchantment with United States foreign and military policies and the natural reluctance of many young men to enter the armed forces have combined to keep a steady stream of draft cases flowing through the courts. In fact, the stream has been so heavy that a new type of legal specialist has recently emerged— the lawyer whose practice is devoted almost exclusively to preventing young men from being drafted.

In Detroit, for example, the law firm of Lafferty, Reosti, Jabara, Papakhian, James and Stickgold handled seven hundred draft cases in less than a year. A partner in the firm, James Lafferty, says any good lawyer can block a client's induction for at least two years with a series of legal maneuvers. Lafferty points out that many of his clients, and thousands of other young men, are woefully uninformed on the possible grounds for deferment available to them. He recalls one case in which he interviewed a young man who faced induction after losing his student deferment. The young man wanted to flee to Canada, which has become a haven for many Americans seeking to evade the draft. "We talked for a while," Lafferty says. "Then I found out that the kid had a child and a blind wife waiting for him outside the office." Without any trouble, Lafferty got the young man an automatic defermen on the ground that his wife and child needed his financial support.

Some lawyers specializing in draft cases say they can virtually guarantee even more than the two years of freedom from induction mentioned by Lafferty. Harry Peck of Milwaukee says: "A person who follows my advice and works hard on developing his case is probably going to stay out of the Army." And William Smith of Los Angeles says that if a youth and his parents can afford $250 a year in fees, "I can give them 99.9 percent assurance that he won't be drafted—and I won't do anything illegal."

If all other avenues have been exhausted by a potential draftee and/or his lawyer, he has two last means of taking his case before the courts. He can go through with his induction and then ask a court to release him from the service on a writ of habeas corpus. He may then present evidence that he has been unjustly drafted. In the alternative, he can refuse induction and face trial on draft evasion charges, but risk a prison term if he does so. Despite the risk, the number of young men refusing induction has soared in recent years. In 1964, the government prosecuted 287 men who had refused induction. By 1968, the number had risen to 3,305.

The tide of cases passing through the courts has resulted in numerous recent rulings substantially broadening the rights of those seeking to avoid the draft by lawful means. A discussion of some of the more significant cases provides useful background information for all potential draftees anxious for protection against unfair treatment.

One of the most difficult issues faced by draft boards and courts considering draft cases concerns conscientious objectors. A conscientious objector is a person whose religious beliefs, personal conscience, or both prevent him from taking up arms, even at the risk of imprisonment. Pacifists and members of certain religious denominations—such as the Seventh-day Adventists, the Quakers, and the Jehovah's Witnesses—usually seek draft deferments as conscientious objectors. In addition, those who are not members of such religious groups but whose past activities show them to be sincere conscientious objectors are generally granted deferments. Such deferments may, however, require the conscientious objector either to enter military service in a noncombatant role—for example, as a medic or ambulance driver—or to perform some other socially useful service outside the military.

The sticky questions in conscientious objection cases usually arise over men who are not members of pacifist religious groups but oppose war or else do not oppose all wars but merely specific ones, such as the Vietnam war. Under various draft laws passed by Congress, conscientious-objector status was supposed to be granted only to men who opposed war on religious grounds. But, in one of the most important cases decided in this field, that provision was challenged by a twenty-two-year-old Harvard University graduate named John Heffron Sisson, Jr.

Sisson opposed war on moral, not religious, grounds. When he applied for conscientious-objector status, his draft board in Boston notified him he was ineligible, since the law limited exemption to someone who "by reason of religious training and belief is conscientiously opposed to participation in war in any form." Not only did Sisson lack the "religious training and belief" required by the law; his conscientious objection was based on specific opposition to the Vietnam war, not necessarily to all wars. Nonetheless, he felt as a matter of conscience that he could not serve in the armed forces, even if his refusal meant he would have to go to prison. As a result, he refused induction in April 1968. A year later, he was convicted of violating the draft law. His lawyers then filed a motion asking U.S. District Judge Charles E. Wyzanski, Jr., to overturn the conviction. They contended it was unconstitutional for the draft law to limit conscientious-objector status to religious opponents of war.

Judge Wyzanski agreed, declaring that the section of the draft law dealing with the subject was indeed unconstitutional, since it discriminated against atheists, agnostics, and those with deep moral convictions.

Judge Wyzanski's ruling, which reversed Sisson's conviction, also was applicable to all similar cases arising in the area served by the federal district courts in Boston. As a practical matter, however, it could be cited as a precedent in any federal court in the United States. Partly as a result of the Wyzanski decision, but even more as a result of opposition to the Vietnam war, the number of young men classified as conscientious objectors has risen dramatically. In 1966, about 7,000 men were classified as conscientious objectors willing to perform civilian work contributing to the national health, safety, or interest. By late 1969, that figure had almost doubled. In addition, there had been a 73-percent increase during the three-year period in the number of conscientious objectors actually performing such civilian work.

A conscientious objector who refuses to perform the required civilian service is subject to imprisonment. In another test case arising in Boston, the right of the government to enforce this provision of the draft law was upheld by the U.S. Court of Appeals for the First Circuit. Richard M. Boardman, a conscientious objector from Acton, Massachusetts, had refused to fulfill the civilian-service requirement. He was convicted of violating the draft law and given a three-year prison term by U.S. District Judge Francis J. W. Ford of Boston. Boardman appealed the conviction to the circuit court, contending that the civilian-service requirement violated his free exercise of religion. His lawyers argued that his refusal to take a job assigned him at a Boston hospital was based on his conviction that such a civilian position was merely an extension of military service. The circuit court rejected this contention and upheld the conviction. It ruled that the federal courts must defer to the judgment of Congress and require conscientious objectors to perform some alternative to military service.

Another of the sensitive problems arising over the draft concerned the rights of young men to protest government policies without being subjected to reprisals through the draft process. In October 1967—disturbed by a wave of antiwar protests that included burning of draft cards, destruction of draft board records, and the like—Selective Service Director Lewis Hershey sent a memorandum to all draft boards urging them to discipline protesters by speeding their inductions as rapidly as Selective Service regulations would permit. Under the regulations then in effect, draft boards were empowered to place at the top of the induction lists the names of any men they considered "delinquent" in abiding by draft procedures. Prior to the issuance of Hershey's memorandum, the "delinquency" provisions had generally been invoked against men who failed to comply with such routine requirements as notifying their draft boards of changes in address, marital status, or deferment eligibility. Hershey's memorandum sought to broaden the "delinquency" provisions to include protest activity. Hershey, long a controversial figure, became even more controversial. Demands for his resignation or ouster were made throughout the country. He refused to back down, however, and remained in office until early 1970 when he retired as Selective Service director, but was named by President Nixon as an adviser on draft policies.

Following issuance of Hershey's memorandum, many draft boards complied with his recommendations and ordered accelerated inductions for draft protesters. Among those affected was David Earl Gutknecht of Minneapolis, Minnesota. In 1967 Gutknecht was classified 1A by his draft board. He requested deferment on the ground that he was a conscientious objector, but the board refused to reclassify him. While he was appealing this decision, he attended an antiwar rally outside the Minneapolis Federal Building. In the course of the demonstration, he tossed his draft card at the feet of a federal marshal. His draft board quickly declared him "delinquent" and, six days later, ordered him drafted. When he refused induction, he was convicted of violating the draft law and sentenced to four years in prison.

The case was appealed to the U.S. Supreme Court, which reversed the conviction on January 19, 1970. In doing so, the court ruled invalid the entire "delinquency" system used by the Selective Service System. It held that draft officials did not have legal power to speed the induction of men for participating in antiwar protests or for such other supposed "delinquencies" as failing to notify their draft boards of address changes, since Congress had never granted them this authority. "There is no suggestion in the current draft law that the Selective Service System has free-wheeling authority to ride herd on the registrants, using immediate induction as a disciplinary or vindictive measure," said the court's unanimous decision.

A week after issuing its ruling in the Gutknecht case, the Supreme Court handed down another far-reaching decision. This decision came in the case of Timothy J. Breen, a twenty-two-year-old college student. Breen held a student deferment until he gave his draft card to a clergyman as an act of protest against the Vietnam war. He was then reclassified 1A. He tried to challenge the reclassification in lower federal courts, but was turned down on the ground that such challenges had specifically been banned by Congress in a 1967 amendment to the draft law. The Supreme Court, however, reversed the lower court rulings. It decided that the 1967 amendment could not be applied to students and that the Selective Service System lacked legal authority to reclassify students 1A as punishment for turning in their draft cards.

In another case, a federal judge in New York ordered a soldier released from the Army on the ground that his draft board had illegally denied him a reclassification hearing before induction. In his decision, Judge Lloyd F. MacMahon caustically criticized what he called "the mind-numbing maze of statutes, regulations, and memoranda" of the Selective Service System. The case involved a former Fordham University law student, Joseph Vaccarino, who had been granted a student deferment. On April 30, 1968, while still attending Fordham, Vaccarino asked his draft board to reclassify him by substituting a 3A hardship deferment for the student deferment. He resided with his father, who was very ill, and an unmarried sister. The draft board refused to reclassify him. Following his graduation from Fordham on July 18, 1968, he was reclassified 1A.

On April 7, 1969, Vaccarino's father died. Under Selective Service regulations, he was required to notify his draft board within ten days of the death that his family status had changed. Apparently unaware of the regulation, he failed to notify the board. Then, when he later asked for a hearing to challenge his 1A status, the board turned him down, claiming he had waived the right to have his case reopened by failing to give notice of his father's death.

Vaccarino was drafted and, in a stroke of irony, assigned to work as a clerk in the main armed forces induction center in New York. His attorneys filed suit, seeking his release from the Army. Judge MacMahon upheld their claim ruling that the draft board had acted illegally in denying Vaccarino a reclassification hearing. The judge severely criticized the Selective Service System for trying to hold potential draftees responsible for complying with numerous technical details.

Even more serious challenges are currently being mounted against the very existence of the draft system. The American Civil Liberties Union is seeking to have the draft outlawed as unconstitutional. And a presidential commission has recommended to President Nixon that the Selective Service System be replaced by an all-volunteer Army, backed by a standby draft for national emergencies. The commission urged that the current draft be eliminated by mid-1971. But federal officials, while supporting the general nature of the commission's recommendations, said it would be impractical to put them into effect as early as 1971.

Thus, for the immediate future at least, young men face continued exposure to the current draft system. Assuming that a young man is drafted, he is normally required to serve two years on active duty. He then must serve an additional four years in military reserve status.

For both men who have been drafted and those who have enlisted voluntarily, military life presents a whole new set of legal requirements. Legal rights that may have been taken for granted in civilian life are suddenly found to be absent or diminished. Historically, it has been assumed that the need for tight military discipline must logically result in depriving members of the armed forces of many rights available to civilians. For years, the U.S. Supreme Court held that the Bill of Rights did not apply to soldiers. In 1867, for example, Chief Justice Salmon P. Chase ruled that "the power of Congress in the government of the land and naval forces . . . is not at all affected by the Fifth or any other amendment."

By and large, the general code of military justice that prevailed during the American Revolution was still in effect through World War II. It was not until 1950 that adoption of the Uniform Code of Military Justice introduced some semblance of due process into the system. There is, besides the issue of fairness of court-martial, the whole range of questions concerning such matters as the military man's freedom of speech (including the right to dissent from government policy), his freedom of assembly, his freedom of the press (through such publications as underground newspapers), and the like. It is in such areas that he has won some of his greatest recent victories—but it is also in such areas that he often feels he still faces his greatest legal obstacles.

As a natural consequence of such civilian developments as the civil rights movement, the peace movement, and the various militant student movements, young military men have banded together in recent years in what might best be termed the G.I. rights movement. On military bases throughout the country and a few abroad, dissident soldiers, sailors, airmen, and Marines have demanded that their commanding officers recognize rights that have long been considered unthinkable by died-in-the-wool military minds. Much of the activity within the G.I. rights movement has centered around opposition to the Vietnam war —an issue that naturally touches raw nerves in the higher echelons of the military, whose members deem it their duty to promote support for the war effort.

Just how difficult the problem has become may be illustrated by a brief summary of recent incidents of dissent within the military, most of them generated by antiwar sentiment, but some by other issues.

In Tacoma, Washington, seventeen soldiers filed a federal court suit asking for protection of their rights of free speech and assembly. The soldiers were among thirty-five G.I.'s arrested by military policemen at Fort Lewis during a meeting of the American Servicemen's Union, a group trying to organize soldiers along the lines of a labor union. The organization's program includes election of military officers, an end to saluting, and recognition of the right to bargain collectively and disobey "illegal" orders.

At Camp Pendleton, California, two Negro Marines urged other Negroes to report to superior officers their feeling that the Vietnam conflict was a "white man's war" in which black men should not be required to fight. They were given military trials that resulted in long prison sentences.

At Fort Dix, New Jersey, a G.I. was convicted by a military court for distributing antiwar literature on the base. In another incident at the same base, thirty-eight prisoners were charged with rioting in the stockade. The riot, which included the burning of mattresses and destruction of furniture, was in protest of conditions in the stockade. Just before the riot, the prisoners were forced to stand in formation for three hours, then stand in line three hours for dinner—only to find there weren't enough dishes for half the men.

At Fort Ord, California, about three hundred prisoners staged a sit-down protest in the stockade. Their protest was aimed at purported brutality by their guards, short rations, and generally primitive living conditions.

At Fort Gordon, Georgia, the Army gave an undesirable discharge to a soldier who edited an antiwar underground newspaper called *The Last Harass*. The officer who recommended his discharge said he felt the newspaper "would have little effect on seasoned officers, but would be dangerous in the case of trainees or men in the Army against their will." At least fifteen other underground newspapers were being published by enlisted men on bases across the country.

In Oakland, California, a Navy nurse was sentenced to six months imprisonment after she took part in a peace demonstration while wearing her uniform.

At Fort Jackson, South Carolina, eight soldiers who belonged to an organization called G.I.'s United Against the War in Vietnam were arrested for speaking against the war during off-duty hours. They filed suit in federal court, seeking to obtain for soldiers the same rights of dissent available to civilians. The Army eventually dropped all charges against the men—an action that prompted their lawyer to call the case "the most important victory to date of the G.I. antiwar movement."

At Cannon Air Force Base, New Mexico, a Negro airman who refused to cut his Afro-style hair was sentenced to ninety days in prison. He served the term, but in the meantime rules were changed to permit such hair styles. Nonetheless, he asked the federal courts to rule on the legality of his conviction on charges of refusing to obey a superior's order. At this writing, the case is still pending.

In various military towns across the country, off-base coffeehouses catering to antiwar G.I.'s and their girlfriends have been opened. In some cases, military authorities have pressured local officials to close the places, on the theory they breed poor morale. But most such efforts have failed.

Perhaps the most highly publicized recent military uprising occurred on October 14, 1968, in the stockade of the Presidio, an Army base in San Francisco. It resulted in twenty-seven soldiers being charged with mutiny. The

Presidio affair was particularly revealing, for it provided unusual insights into the way the Army recruits its men, the way it handles its misfits, the way it deals with grievances, and the way it dispenses justice.

The average age of the men charged with mutiny was nineteen. Most of them came from small towns or medium-sized cities, where they had been high school dropouts. Many of them enlisted in the Army after being promised useful vocational training. Private Stephen Rowland, for example, enlisted to be trained as an occupational therapist; Private Danny Wilkins was told he'd be given computer training. Once in the Army, however, they found that the promises were not to be kept. Not one of the men was given the vocational training assignment he expected. Their discontent was heightened by the tough discipline imposed by drill sergeants and other superiors. Under the unaccustomed pressure of military life, and the resentment of broken promises, the response of many of the men was to try to run away from the Army. They went AWOL (away without leave), an offense the Army takes very seriously.

The problem of AWOL soldiers has become increasingly severe during the Vietnam war. In 1968, a Senate committee reported, 208,893 soldiers went AWOL or deserted from the Army. To cope with the problem, the Army has abandoned its previous policy of allowing obviously disturbed misfits to be discharged from the service. Instead, it now imprisons them in stockades. As a result, stockades on bases throughout the country are filled beyond capacity with men who would probably be troublesome even under ideal conditions. The conditions in most stockades are far from ideal. Not only are they overcrowded; many of them are filthy, deteriorated buildings supervised by guards who delight in harassing and sometimes beating prisoners.

At the Presidio, conditions were perhaps worse than the average stockade. The building in which the accused mutineers were housed was built in 1912 to accommodate 43 persons. The Army now considers its normal capacity to be eighty-eight. But, for the two months preceding the uprising, it contained more than 100 prisoners. On the day of the purported mutiny, there were 123 prisoners jammed inside. "The tension brought on by being unable to move without dodging other prisoners is enormous," says one former Presidio inmate.

In addition to the crowded conditions, there were other sources of discomfort. The building had only four latrines, whose plumbing was out of order almost as often as not. To go to the bathroom or take a shower, a prisoner frequently was forced to wait in line for more than two hours. Food was short, and prisoners complained it was barely edible. Guards, armed with shotguns, taunted and threatened prisoners. Thus, the Presidio had most of the ingredients necessary for an explosion of human emotions. All that was needed was some spark to touch off the explosion.

The spark was provided by a tragic incident involving a nineteen-year-old private named Richard Bunch. A small man—5 feet 4 inches, 120 pounds—Bunch was pitied by his fellow prisoners at the stockade. They considered him insane and felt he belonged in a mental hospital. Bunch had deserted from the Army, spent months taking LSD, and then returned to his home in Ohio. His mother notified Army officials that he was home and appeared mentally ill. The Army promised her in writing that it would give her

[165]

son psychiatric treatment. Instead, it sent him to the stockade.

There, his fellow inmates quickly decided he was deranged. It didn't take much perception on their part. Bunch sat on his bunk in a lotus position much of the time, mumbling that he was a warlock and could kill people with a glance. Often, he would announce that he could walk through walls and would then walk into them. At night, Bunch's frantic screaming awakened virtually everyone in the stockade. But no move was made by the authorities to give him the promised psychiatric treatment.

In early October 1968, Bunch asked a fellow prisoner to recommend a foolproof method of committing suicide. The other man suggested trying to run away from the guards, who were armed with shotguns, while on a work detail. In the next few days Bunch wrote a series of barely coherent notes, clearly hinting at suicide.

On October 11, while on a work detail, Bunch asked a guard: "If I run, will you shoot me?"

"You'll have to run to find out," the guard replied.

"Well, be sure to shoot me in the head."

With that, Bunch began walking, then skipping, then trotting away from the guard. When he had gone barely thirty feet, the guard fired a 12-gauge shotgun blast directly at his back. Although Army regulations specify that guards should fire only as a last resort and then aim for the legs, this blast struck Bunch in the heart, lungs, kidney, and spleen. It left a hole the size of a grapefruit in his back. After shooting Bunch, the guard turned on another prisoner, pointed the gun at him, and shouted: "Hit the ground. Hit the ground or I'll shoot you, too." In all that time, none of the witnesses ever heard the guard order Bunch to halt.

Bunch was dead by the time anyone reached his crumpled form. Word of the shooting spread quickly through the stockade, bringing the prisoners' anger to fever pitch. Then came the final straw. Army officials conducted a hurry-up investigation, concluding that the guard had actually aimed for Bunch's legs but that his shotgun had malfunctioned and fired higher than intended. They ruled the slaying a case of "justifiable homicide," and pressed no charges against the guard.

The inmates decided that was more than they could stomach. Some of them discussed the possibility of killing a guard or burning down the stockade. But calmer heads prevailed, and it was decided instead to stage a nonviolent, orderly protest aimed at getting someone in authority to listen to their grievances.

A list of demands was compiled. It included elimination of shotgun guards on work details; complete psychological evaluation of all prisoners and guards; improved sanitary facilities; better food; rotation of guards to curb development of antagonism between guards and inmates; and an opportunity to tell the press the prisoners' version of the Bunch shooting.

By prearrangement, when the roll of prisoners was called at 7:30 A.M. on October 14, twenty-seven of the inmates broke ranks and sat down in a grassy area of the stockade. They asked to see Captain Robert S. Lamont, the stockade commander. Lamont arrived a few minutes later, accompanied by a fire truck and an Army photographer who began taking pictures of the demonstrators. One of the inmates, Private Walter Pawlowski, stood up and started to read the list of demands. Lamont cut him off. He walked over to a loudspeaker and proceeded to read Article 94 of the Uniform Code of Military Justice—the mutiny article, which provides a possible death penalty for violators. "Any person subject to this code who, with intent to usurp or override lawful military authority, refuses, in concert with any other person, to obey orders or otherwise do his duty or creates any violence or disturbance, is guilty of mutiny," Lamont recited.

Up to that point, the demonstrators had disobeyed no orders. Lamont, in first approaching the men, had not ordered them to disperse. When he took to the loudspeaker, the men tried drowning him out. They sang *We Shall Overcome, America the Beautiful* and *This Land Is My Land*. They chanted demands for freedom, for visits by news reporters, and for a chance to confer with Terence Hallinan, a San Francisco lawyer who represented several prisoners. Amid this din, Lamont did order the men to return to their barracks—but whether they heard him is a subject of dispute.

After about forty minutes, Lamont asked the chief of the fire truck to turn a hose on the demonstrators. The chief, a civilian, refused. Lamont then directed twenty-five Military Policemen to remove the demonstrators. They did so, without having to resort to force. A few prisoners refused to walk away and had to be carried. But, otherwise, there was no physical resistance.

Then began an exercise of military justice typical of many others, the sort that brings frequent complaints of unfairness. Under the Uniform Code of Military Justice, the commanding officer of a soldier's unit is entitled to bring charges against him, appoint his military defense counsel, select the court-martial panel (jury), and even approve or disapprove the verdict and sentence. In civilian terms, this system would be the virtual equivalent of hav-. ing one man serve as prosecutor, judge, and jury—with veto power over the defense lawyers.

In the Presidio case, the commanding officer was Lieutenant General Stanley R. Larsen, commander of the Sixth Army (headquartered at the Presidio). Larsen, as required by the military justice code, ordered a pretrial hearing. He appointed Captain Richard J. Millard as hearing officer, with responsibility for examining the facts and making recommendations on how the Army should proceed against the prisoners. Millard's hearing convinced him that Captain Lamont had been wrong in charging the prisoners with mutiny.

Millard recommended that the Army abandon the mutiny charges, with their possible death penalty, and prosecute the demonstrators instead on lesser charges that could bring a maximum sentence of six months or separation from the Army with less than an honorable discharge. Other subordinates of General Larsen also urged him to drop the mutiny charges. But the general apparently was determined to make an example of the Presidio men—to show other soldiers that dissent would not be tolerated under his command. He ordered the men tried for mutiny.

The resulting trials created a furor. Evidence of brutality by guards and intolerable living conditions in the stockade received broad publicity. Fifteen prominent psychiatrists, summoned by Terence Hallinan as civilian defense counsel, testified that such conditions were bound to create rebellious behavior among prisoners. While the

[169]

trials were in progress, protests similar to the Presidio demonstration—some of them much more violent—erupted at military bases in Kansas, Colorado, Texas, New Jersey, and elsewhere in California.

When the first three demonstrators to come to trial received prison sentences of fourteen, fifteen, and sixteen years respectively, the national uproar grew in intensity. The Army Judge Advocate General's Office in Washington felt compelled to reduce the sentences to two years each. But, even so, the ferment persisted. The sentencing of other demonstrators to lesser terms did little to remedy the situation. Demands were heard in Congress and elsewhere for major reforms in the entire military justice system. Prominent Americans spoke out in favor of broadening the rights of servicemen across the board, bringing them more in line with the rights available to civilians.

Ultimately, the Army bowed to the pressure. It issued a memorandum to its commanding officers, entitled *Guidance on Dissent,* that substantially expanded the rights of soldiers. The memorandum—dealing with such subjects as demonstrations by servicemen, distribution of political literature on military bases, underground newspapers, coffeehouses, and servicemen's unions—instructed commanding officers "to impose only such minimum restraints as are necessary to enable the Army to perform its mission." The memorandum, among other things, requires the following:

1. That a commanding officer not prevent the distribution of a publication "simply because he does not like its contents. . . . A commander must have cogent reasons for any denial of distribution privileges. The fact that a publi-

cation is critical—even unfairly critical—of government policies or officials is not in itself a ground for denial."

2. That a commanding officer telephone Army headquarters in Washington and request approval before prohibiting distribution of any publication.

3. That a commander may not prohibit the possession of "an unauthorized publication." Possession, coupled with an attempt to distribute the publication in violation of base regulations, however, may constitute an offense.

4. That a commander recognize that membership in a servicemen's union is not against Army regulations, although commanders "are not authorized to recognize or bargain with such a union."

5. That a commander not prevent his men from going to a coffeehouse "unless it can be shown, for example, that activities taking place in the coffeehouse include counseling soldiers to refuse to perform duty or to desert or otherwise involve illegal acts with a significant adverse effect on soldier health, morale or welfare."

6. That a commander may not discipline soldiers who work off base, on their own time and with their own money, on underground newspapers, unless the newspapers contain material that is punishable under federal law.

7. That a commander may not arbitrarily deny civilians a permit to demonstrate on the base. He may deny the permit if he can show, for example, that the demonstration would endanger loyalty, discipline, and morale.

The memorandum noted that "it is important to recognize that the question of 'soldier dissent' is linked with the constitutional right of free speech and that the Army's reaction to such dissent will—quite properly—continue to receive much attention in the news media." Any military action at any level dealing with dissent, it continued, "may therefore reflect, either favorably or adversely, on the image of the Army with the American public."

While setting guidelines, the memorandum left the ultimate decision, except in the banning of a publication, with the individual commander. But it warned commanders to beware of overreacting to specific incidents of dissent. "Severe disciplinary action in response to a relatively insignificant manifestation of dissent can have a counter-productive effect on other members of the command because the reaction appears out of proportion to the threat which the dissent represents," the memorandum cautioned. "Thus, rather than serving as a deterrent, such disproportionate actions may stimulate further breaches of discipline."

Although the memorandum applied only to Army commanders, similar policies were put into effect by other branches of the military. In addition, several court decisions served to further broaden the legal rights of servicemen. The U.S. Supreme Court, for example, ruled in 1969 that servicemen could not be court-martialed in peacetime for alleged crimes committed off military bases within the United States. They would thus be tried in civilian courts, with the same legal rights available to civilians.

Despite such expansion of their rights, many servicemen still feel they are being short-changed. To gain further advances, representatives of various servicemen's groups met in Washington in late 1969 for a National Conference on G.I. Rights. Among the sponsors of the conference were the Chicago and New York branches of Veterans for Peace in Vietnam, the American Servicemen's Union, G.I.'s United

Against the War in Vietnam, Servicemen's Link to Peace, and the G.I. Civil Liberties Defense Committee. The two-day conference ended with the formation of a "G.I. lobby" —a group assigned to pressure government officials in Washington and elsewhere for continued extension of legal rights to servicemen.

It seems apparent that, although servicemen still do not enjoy some of the rights they would like, they have made significant gains in recent years. And both the machinery and the public climate exist for further gains in the immediate future.

SUMMARY

1. All American males must register for the draft at the age of eighteen. They must carry their Selective Service cards and, when classified, their classification cards with them when outside their homes or face the possibility of imprisonment and/or fines.

2. Various means are available to obtain deferments from military service—for example, medical or mental disability; student status; family responsibilities (in some cases), and conscientious-objector status. Increasingly large numbers of young men are obtaining conscientious-objector deferments. It is now possible for them to claim such deferments even if their objections to war are based on moral, rather than religious, grounds.

3. Servicemen, like many young civilians, are rebelling against the authority of the government. To cope with such rebellion, the military services are relaxing their rules to permit greater dissent in the form of unorthodox haircuts, underground newspapers, off-base coffeehouses for antiwar advocates, etc. But servicemen still are denied numerous rights available to civilians.

4. The system of military justice, long subject to sharp criticism, is undergoing reforms aimed at giving servicemen legal rights more in accord with those of civilians accused of breaking the law.

IN CONCLUSION

A book such as this cannot pretend to be the final word on such a complex subject as the legal rights of young people. Events are moving so swiftly that today's prescriptions are soon as dated as the magazines in a doctor's office. Moreover, a legal right granted in one section of the country may well be denied in another. The most an author of this sort of book can do is try to point out the national trends, so that young people have guidelines to indicate what they may prudently demand and how they may expect to be treated.

The trends, as described, are clearly in the direction of broadening young people's rights. At the same time, there are—and undoubtedly will continue to be—many adults determined to limit, perhaps even narrow, the rights of their juniors. While minors can justly continue to press for further advances, it would be wise for them to concentrate on goals within reach of attainment. In some cases, outlandish demands do much more harm than good. They prevent young people from obtaining rights that might otherwise be available to them.

A final word remains to be said. Rights bring with them responsibilities. The best way for a young person to refute the argument that he is not yet ready for full exercise of his rights is to deal responsibly with those he has and to demonstrate, even when seeking new rights, that he is serious, not frivolous, in making his demands.

APPENDICES

A

EXCERPTS FROM
"RIGHTS AND RESPONSIBILITIES
FOR SENIOR HIGH SCHOOL STUDENTS,"
ISSUED BY THE NEW YORK CITY BOARD OF EDUCATION

1. In each high school there should be established an elective and truly representative student government with offices open to all students in good standing. All students should be allowed to vote. This government should be elected annually. The student government shall have the power to allocate student activity funds, subject to established audit controls and the by-laws of the board of education. It shall also participate in making decisions in certain areas, including curriculum and disciplinary policies. The representatives chosen by the student government shall meet at least monthly with the principal to exchange views, to share in the formulation of school student policies, to discuss faculty-student relations and any other matters of student concern.

2. A parent-student-faculty council, as established by previous board of education resolutions, shall meet monthly with the principal to discuss matters of common interest, make recommendations and to insure implementation of agreed-upon innovations.

3. Official school publications shall reflect the policy and judgment of the student editors. This entails the obligation

to be governed by the standards of responsible journalism, such as avoidance of libel, obscenity and defamation. Student publications shall provide as much opportunity as possible for the sincere expression of student opinion.

4. Students may exercise their constitutionally protected rights of free speech and assembly so long as they do not interfere with the operations of the regular school program. Students have a right to wear political buttons, armbands and other badges of symbolic expression. Students may distribute political leaflets, newspapers and other literature, without prior authorization, at locations adjacent to the school. Students shall be allowed to distribute leaflets, newspapers and other literature, with prior authorization, at specified locations and times designated within the school for that purpose. No commercial material, no obscene material and nothing advocating racial or religious prejudice shall be permitted to be distributed within the school. In noting these exceptions, it is clearly the intention of the board of education to promote the dissemination of diverse viewpoints and to foster discussion of all political and social issues. Decisions under this section restricting the distribution of literature within the school shall be made by the principal or with his agreement by some other body which shall consist of students and faculty. . . . Students may form political and social organizations, including those that champion unpopular causes, provided they are open to all students and governed by the regulations pertaining to student government regarding extracurricular activities. These organizations shall have reasonable access to school facilities.

5. Students have the right to determine their own dress, except where such dress is clearly dangerous or is so dis-

tractive as to clearly interfere with the learning and teaching process. This right may not be restricted, even by a dress code arrived at by a majority vote of students. . . .

6. Students have the right to receive annually, upon the opening of school, a publication setting forth all the rules and regulations to which students are subject. This publication shall also include a statement of the rights granted to students. It shall be distributed to parents as well.

7. Students shall have the right to a fair hearing, as provided for in the State Education Law, which includes "representation by counsel with the right to question witnesses against such pupils," prior to any disciplinary action which could result in suspension from classes for more than five days.

8. Any decision concerning student rights and responsibilities by school personnel is subject to discussion by the consultative council [composed of students, parents and faculty members]. Appeals from the decisions of the head of the school must first be lodged with the assistant superintendent in charge of the high schools, then the chancellor and finally the central board of education. All such appeals shall be decided as quickly as possible.

B

EXCERPTS FROM
"JOINT STATEMENT ON
RIGHTS AND FREEDOMS OF STUDENTS,"
ISSUED BY TRINITY UNIVERSITY, SAN ANTONIO, TEXAS

The professor in the classroom and in conference should encourage free discussion, inquiry and expression. Student performance should be evaluated solely on an academic basis, not on opinions or conduct outside of class in matters unrelated to academic standards. Students shall be free to take reasoned exception to the data or views offered in any course of study and to reserve judgment about matters of opinion, but they are responsible for learning the content of any course of study for which they are enrolled as well as acquiring and demonstrating the skills and competencies required. . . .

Recognizing that students should have protection through orderly procedures against prejudice or capricious academic evaluation and recognizing that they are responsible for maintaining standards of academic performance, Trinity University adheres to . . . procedures for such protection. [These procedures permit a student who believes he has received an unfair grade to appeal first to the

Courtesy: Trinity University, San Antonio, Texas

[182]

professor involved, then to the chairman of the appropriate department, and finally to a faculty review committee.]

Information about student views, beliefs and political associations which professors acquire in the course of their work . . . shall be considered confidential. Protection against improper disclosure is a serious professional obligation. Judgments of ability and character may be provided under appropriate circumstances involving the education of professional interests of students. . . . No records shall be kept which reflect the political activities or beliefs of students. . . .

Students bring to the campus a variety of interests previously acquired and develop many new interests as members of the academic community. They shall be free to organize and join associations. . . . The membership, policies and actions of a student organization will be determined by a vote of only those persons who are registered as students in Trinity University. . . . Each organization should be free to choose its own adviser from the university community. Campus advisers may advise organizations in the exercise of responsibility, but they shall not have the authority to control the policies of such organizations. . . .

Students and student organizations shall be free to examine and discuss all questions of interest to them, and to express opinions publicly and privately. They shall be free to support causes by orderly means which do not disrupt the regular operations of Trinity University. At the same time, students and student organizations must make clear to the academic and larger community that they speak only for themselves in their public expressions or demonstrations, and do not necessarily express the views of Trinity University.

Student organizations shall be allowed to invite and to hear any person of their own choosing provided that regular operations, institutional property and personal safety are not endangered thereby and provided that they follow the approved procedures for scheduling such speakers. These uniform procedures shall be drawn up in cooperation between faculty, administration and the Trinity University Student Association, and shall be published in a handbook which shall be available to all members of the academic community. . . .

As constituents of the academic community, students should be free, individually and collectively, to express their views on issues of institutional policy and on matters of general interest to the student body. Students, individually and collectively, have the right to petition any faculty or administrative committee to express their opinions and views on matters which concern them. Committees which deal directly with student activities shall have student representatives on their membership with full voting power. These include, under the present structure, at least the following administrative committees of the university and on these duly appointed students should comprise not less than one-fifth of the committee membership: Administrative Council, Admissions Committee, Calendar Committee, Board of Publications, Religious Life and Work Committee. To further insure the ability of students to express opinions on institutional policy, at least one student representative may be appointed to serve on the following committees as nonvoting advisory members: Athletic Council, Curriculum Committee, Library Committee, Scholarship and Student Aid Committee. . . . Student representatives will be chosen by the Student Council. . . .

The student press shall be responsible to the university under the supervision and direction of a Board of Publications composed of an equal number of students and faculty-staff representatives. Within the broad guidelines established by the Board of Publications, the student press shall be free of censorship, and its editors and managers shall be free to develop their own editorial policies and news coverage.

The editorial freedom of student editors and managers necessitates corollary responsibility governed by the canons of responsible journalism such as avoidance of libel, indecency, undocumented allegations, attacks on personal integrity and techniques of harassment and innuendo. . . . Only for proper and stated causes may editors and managers be subject to removal from office by orderly and prescribed procedures as set by the Board of Publications. Editors and managers of student publications shall be free from arbitrary suspension and removal because of student, faculty, administrative or public disapproval of editorial policy or content. . . .

Trinity University students are both citizens and members of the academic community. As citizens they shall enjoy the same freedom of speech, peaceful assembly, the right of petition that other citizens enjoy, and as members of the academic community they are subject to the obligations which accrue to them by virtue of membership. Institutional powers shall not be employed to inhibit such intellectual and personal development of students as is often promoted by their exercise of the rights of citizenship both on and off campus. Activities of students may, upon occasion, result in violation of the law, but this in itself does not constitute a basis for additional penalties by the university. However, the university may impose penalties independent of and in addition to the actions of a civil or circuit court when its own community interests are affected. . . .

In developing responsible student conduct, disciplinary proceedings play a role substantially secondary to example, counseling guidance and admonition. At the same time, Trinity University recognizes its responsibility to protect its institutional purpose by setting standards of scholarship, conduct and use of its facilities. Proper procedural safeguards shall be observed to protect the student from imposition of unfair penalties in all situations. Procedural fair play recognizes that the student at Trinity University be informed of the nature of the charges against him, that he be given a fair opportunity to refute them, that Trinity University not be arbitrary in its actions and that there be provisions for appeal of a decision. . . .

Disciplinary proceedings shall be instituted only for infractions of standards of conduct which should be set forth in the Trinity University Student Handbook and available to all students. Offenses, along with maximum penalties, shall be clearly defined and reasonably applied. Major standards of conduct, the violation of which may lead to suspension or expulsion from the university, shall be formulated by a committee composed of the dean of the university, the dean and associate dean of student life, two faculty members nominated and elected by the faculty and three students chosen by the Student Council. . . .

Except under extreme circumstances, rooms or premises occupied by students and personal possessions of students shall not be searched unless appropriate authorization has been obtained in writing. Any such application must be cleared by the dean or associate dean of student life, and must specify the reasons for the search and the objects and information sought. The student should be present, if possible, during the search.

C

EXCERPTS ON FREEDOM OF THE PRESS FROM "ACADEMIC FREEDOM IN THE SECONDARY SCHOOLS," PUBLISHED BY THE AMERICAN CIVIL LIBERTIES UNION

The preparation and publication of newspapers and magazines is an exercise in freedom of the press. Generally speaking, students should be permitted and encouraged to join together to produce such publications as they wish. Faculty advisers should serve as consultants on style, grammar, format and suitability of the materials. Neither the faculty advisers nor the principal should prohibit the publication or distribution of material except when such publication or distribution would clearly endanger the health or safety of the students, or clearly and imminently threaten to disrupt the educational process, or might be of a libelous nature. Such judgment, however, should never be exercised because of disapproval or disagreement with the article in question.

The school administration and faculty should ensure that students and faculty may have their views represented in the columns of the (official) school newspaper. Where feasible, they should permit the publication of multiple and competing periodicals. These might be produced by the student government, by various clubs, by a class or group of classes, or by individuals banded together for this specific purpose. The material and equipment for publication—such as duplicating machines, paper and ink—should be available to students in such quantity as budget may permit.

The freedom to express one's opinion goes hand in hand with the responsibility for the published statement. The onus of decision as to the content of a publication should be placed clearly on the student editorial board of the particular publication. The editors should be encouraged through practice to learn to judge literary value, newsworthiness and propriety.

The right to offer copies of their work to fellow students should be accorded equally to those who have received school aid and to those whose publications have relied on their own resources (such as underground papers).

The student press should be considered a learning device. Its pages should not be looked upon as an official image of the school, always required to present a polished appearance to the extramural world. Learning effectively proceeds through trial and error, and as much or more may sometimes be gained from reactions to a poor article or a tasteless publication as from the traditional pieces, groomed carefully for external inspection.

D

EXCERPTS ON DUE PROCESS FROM "ACADEMIC FREEDOM IN THE SECONDARY SCHOOLS," PUBLISHED BY THE AMERICAN CIVIL LIBERTIES UNION

The regulations concerning appropriate student behavior in the school at large should preferably be formulated by a student-faculty committee. . . . Regulations governing the school as a whole should be fully and clearly formulated, published and made available to all members of the school community. They should be reasonable. . . .

To maintain the orderly administration of the school, minor infractions of school discipline may be handled in a summary fashion. In every case, a student should be informed of the nature of the infraction with which he is charged. The teacher and/or administrator should bear in mind that an accusation is not the equivalent of guilt, and he should therefore be satisfied of the guilt of the accused student prior to subjecting such student to disciplinary action.

A student's locker should not be opened without his consent except in conformity with the spirit of the Fourth Amendment, which requires that a warrant first be obtained on a showing of probable cause, supported by oath or affirmation, and particularly describing the things to be seized. An exception may be made in cases involving a clear danger to health or safety.

The penalties meted out for breaches of school regulations should be commensurate with the offense. They should never take the form of corporal (that is, physical) punishment. Punishment for infractions of the code of behavior should bear no relation to courses, credits, marks, graduation or similar academic areas, except in cases where they relate to academic dishonesty.

Those infractions which may lead to more serious penalties, such as suspension or expulsion from school, or a notation on the record, require the utilization of a comprehensive and formal procedure in order to prevent a miscarriage of justice that could have serious effects on the student and his future. Such hearings should therefore be approached not in terms of meting out punishment, but rather as an attempt to find the best solution for the student's needs consistent with the maintenance of order in the school.

The procedure should include a formal hearing and the right of appeal. Regulations and proceedings governing the operation of the hearing panel and the appeal should be predetermined in consultation with the students, published and disseminated or otherwise made available to the student body. Responsibility for the decision reached as a result of the hearing rests solely with the administration. It may seek the opinions and participation of teachers and students in reaching its conclusion.

Prior to the hearing, the student (and his parent or guardian) should be: Advised in writing of the charges against him, including a summary of the evidence on which the charges are based; advised that he is entitled to be represented and/or advised at all times during the course of the proceedings by a person of his choosing who may or may not be connected with . . . the school; advised of the procedure to be followed at the hearing; given a reasonable time to prepare his defense.

At the hearing, the student (his parent, guardian or other representative) and the administrator should have the right to examine and cross-examine witnesses and to present documentary and other evidence in support of their respective contentions. The student should be advised of his right to remain silent, and should not be disciplined for claiming this privilege. . . . A full record should be taken at the hearing and it should be made available in identical form to the hearing panel, the administration and the student.

In those instances where the student is being exposed to a serious penalty because of an accumulation of minor infractions which had been handled in summary fashion, or any instance where evidence of prior infractions so handled is presented at the hearing by the administration, the student should be permitted to reopen those charges and present evidence in support of the contention that he was wrongfully accused and/or convicted of the minor infraction.

After the hearing is closed, the panel should adjudicate the matter with reasonable promptness and make its findings in writing. . . . Punishments should, so far as possible, avoid public humiliation or embarrassment. Group punishment should be used only if every member of the group is guilty of the infraction. Cruel and unusual punishment should never be imposed.

E

DRIVERS LICENSES:
AGE REQUIREMENTS BY STATE

State	Learners Permit	Operators License MINIMUM AGE				
		UNLIMITED OPERATION				
	Minimum Age	No Special Provisions	Special* Provisions for Minors	Restricted Operation for Minors*	Motorcycle*	Motorscooter*
Alabama	15	16	—	—	—	14
Alaska	14	18	16	—	—	14
Arizona	15 years and 7 mos.	18	16	—	16	—
Arkansas	14	18	16	—	—	13
California	15½	18	16	14	16	—
Colorado	15½*	18	16	—	16	16
Connecticut	16	21	16	—	16	16
Delaware	16	18	16	—	16	16
Florida	15	18	16	—	—	15
Georgia	15	16	—	—	—	—
Hawaii	15	20	15	—	15	15
Idaho	14*	18	16	14	—	—
Illinois	15–18	21	18	15	18	16
Indiana	15*	21	16	—	—	—
Iowa	14	18	16	14	16	16
Kansas	14	16	—	14	14	14
Kentucky	16	18	16	—	16	16
Louisiana	15	21	15	15	15	15
Maine	15*	18	17	15	16	16
Maryland	16*	21	16	—	16	16
Massachusetts	16	18	—	16½	16½	16½

[193]

DRIVERS LICENSES:
AGE REQUIREMENTS BY STATE

State	Learners Permit	Operators License				
		MINIMUM AGE				
		UNLIMITED OPERATION				
	Minimum Age	No Special Provisions	Special* Provisions for Minors	Restricted Operation for Minors*	Motorcycle*	Motorscooter*
Michigan	16	18	16	14	—	15
Minnesota	15*	18	16	15	15	15
Mississippi	15	17	15	—	—	—
Missouri	15*	16	—	—	16	16
Montana	15*	18	15	13	13	13
Nebraska	15	16	—	14	16	16
Nevada	15½	18	16	14	16	14
New Hampshire	15	18	16	16	16	16
New Jersey	17	17	—	16	17	17
New Mexico	14*	18	15	—	15	13
New York	16	18	17	16	16	16
North Carolina	15½*	18	16	—	—	—
North Dakota	14*	18	16	14	16	16
Ohio	16	21	16	14	16	16
Oklahoma	15½*	16	—	—	—	14
Oregon	15	18	16	14	16	16
Pennsylvania	16	18	17	16	16	16
Rhode Island	16	18	16	—	16	16
South Carolina	15	21	16	15	15	15
South Dakota	14	18	16	14	14	14
Tennessee	16	18	16	—	16	14
Texas	15*	18	15	—	15	15
Utah	16	18	16	—	16	16
Vermont	15	21	18	16	16	16
Virginia	15 years and 8 mos.	18	16	—	16	16

DRIVERS LICENSES:
AGE REQUIREMENTS BY STATE

State	Learners Permit	Operators License MINIMUM AGE				
		UNLIMITED OPERATION				
	Minimum Age	No Special Provisions	Special* Provisions for Minors	Restricted Operation for Minors*	Motor-cycle*	Motor-scooter*
Washington	15*	21	16	—	16	—
West Virginia	16*	18	16	—	—	—
Wisconsin	14*	18	16	14	16	—
Wyoming	15	21	16	—	—	15
District of Columbia	16	18	16	—	16	16

* Qualified by certain restrictions which can be obtained in detail from individual state licensing agencies.

Courtesy: U. S. Department of Transportation.

F

ALCOHOLIC BEVERAGE CONTROL LAWS
CONCERNING MINIMUM AGE REQUIREMENTS

State	Drinking Age Distilled Spirits	Wine	Beer	Legality of Providing and Allowing Minor to Drink Alcoholic Beverages
Alabama	21	21	21	No provision
Alaska	21	21	21	Parent may give to child
Arizona	21	21	21	No provision
Arkansas	21	21	21	No provision
California	21	21	21	No provision
Colorado	21	21	18 for 3.2% Beer 21 other	With parents' consent at home
Connecticut	21	21	21	With parents' consent at home
Delaware	21	21	21	Under no circumstances
District of Columbia	21	21 over 14 % 18 under	18	Illegal
Florida	21	21	21	Illegal
Georgia	21	21	21	With written consent of parent
Hawaii	20	20	20	No provision
Idaho	21	21	20	No provision
Illinois	21	21	21	No provision
Indiana	21	21	21	No provision—unless in reg. armed services
Iowa	21	21	21	Beer—in private home with parents' consent Other—any place by consent of parent, physician, or dentist for medicinal use

ALCOHOLIC BEVERAGE CONTROL LAWS
CONCERNING MINIMUM AGE REQUIREMENTS

| State | Drinking Age | | | Legality of Providing and Allowing Minor to Drink Alcoholic Beverages |
	Distilled Spirits	Wine	Beer	
Kansas	21	21	18 for 3.2% or under— 21 over 3.2%	No provision
Kentucky	21	21	21	None (in licensed premises)
Louisiana	18/21	18/21	18	None
Maine	20	20	20	With parents' consent if over 16
Maryland	21	21	21	No provision
Massachusetts	21	21	21	No provision
Michigan	21	21	21	By a physician
Minnesota	21	21	21	No provision—3.2% (in presence of parents)
Mississippi	21	18	18	No provision
Missouri	21	21	21	With parents' consent at home
Montana	21	21	21	By physician or for sacramental purpose
Nebraska	20	20	20	Illegal
Nevada	21	21	21	No provision
New Hampshire	21	21	21	None
New Jersey	21	21	21	If acquired as gift; not on licensed premises
New Mexico	21	21	21	Only in presence of parent or guardian
New York	18	18	18	No provision
North Carolina	21	21 (17 if married)	18	No provision
North Dakota	21	21	21	If given by parent
Ohio	21	21	18—3.2% 21—6%	Home use only, or by physician
Oklahoma	21	21	21	No provision

ALCOHOLIC BEVERAGE CONTROL LAWS
CONCERNING MINIMUM AGE REQUIREMENTS

State	Drinking Age Distilled Spirits	Wine	Beer	Legality of Providing and Allowing Minor to Drink Alcoholic Beverages
Oregon	21	21	21	With parents' consent at home
Pennsylvania	21	21	21	With parents' consent at home
Rhode Island	21	21	21	Not legal on licensed premises
South Carolina	21	18—14% or under	18	In parents' presence
South Dakota	21	21	21—over 3.2% 19—3.2%	No provision
Tennessee	21	21	21	Under no circumstances
Texas	21	21	21	In presence of parent, guardian, or spouse
Utah	21	21	21	For medicinal purposes by parent, guardian, or doctor
Vermont	21	21	21	With parents' consent at home
Virginia	21	21	21 18—3.2%	No provision
Washington	21	21	21	By parent, guardian, or doctor
West Virginia	21	21	21 18—3.2%	Under no circumstances
Wisconsin	21	21	18	Beer—in presence of parent or guardian
Wyoming	21	21	21	No provision

Courtesy: Licensed Beverage Industries, Inc.

G

MARRIAGE AGE REQUIREMENTS

State	With Consent		Without Consent	
	Men	Women	Men	Women
Alabama	17	14	21	18
Alaska	18	16	21	18
Arizona	18	16	21	18
Arkansas	18	16	21	18
California	18	16	21	18
Colorado	16	16	21	18
Connecticut	16	16	21	21
Delaware	18	16	19	19
District of Columbia	18	16	21	21
Florida	18	16	21	21
Georgia	18	16	19	19
Hawaii	18	16	20	20
Idaho	18	16	21	18
Illinois	18	16	21	18
Indiana	18	16	21	18
Iowa	18	16	21	18
Kansas	18	18	21	18
Kentucky	18	16	18	18
Louisiana	18	16	21	21
Maine	16	16	21	18
Maryland	18	16	21	18
Massachusetts	18	16	21	18
Michigan	18	16	18	18
Minnesota	18	16	21	18
Mississippi	17	15	21	21
Missouri	15	15	21	18
Montana	18	16	21	18
Nebraska	18	16	21	21
Nevada	18	16	21	18
New Hampshire	14	13	20	18

MARRIAGE AGE REQUIREMENTS

	With Consent		Without Consent	
State	*Men*	*Women*	*Men*	*Women*
New Jersey	18	16	21	18
New Mexico	18	16	21	18
New York	16	14	21	18
North Carolina	16	16	18	18
North Dakota	18	15	21	18
Ohio	18	16	21	21
Oklahoma	18	15	21	18
Oregon	18	15	21	18
Pennsylvania	16	16	21	21
Rhode Island	18	16	21	21
South Carolina	16	14	18	18
South Dakota	18	16	21	21
Tennessee	16	16	21	21
Texas	16	14	19	18
Utah	16	14	21	18
Vermont	18	14	21	18
Virginia	18	16	21	21
Washington	17	17	21	18
West Virginia	18	16	21	21
Wisconsin	18	16	21	18
Wyoming	18	16	21	21

Source: *World Almanac*, 1970.

INDEX

ACKNOWLEDGMENTS

I am indebted to George Nicholson, Barbara Seuling, Ross Claiborne, Sandra Scott, and Dorothy Markinko for counsel, faith, and patience.

I would also like to express my appreciation to the many people who provided information and guidance on a difficult subject. Particularly, thanks to the capable personnel of the American Civil Liberties Union, the Council of State Governments, the National Governors' Conference, the U.S. Department of Justice, the Administrative Office of United States Courts, and the President's Commission on Law Enforcement and Administration of Justice.

As always, thanks are due to my wife, Jeanne, and daughters, Pamela and Patricia, for putting up with the deprivations and frustrations of sharing a home with a cantankerous writer.